GROWING UP
STRONG

Empowering Young Minds to Manage EMOTIONS, Navigate CONFLICT, and Embrace GROWTH

ALLISON EDWARDS

NATIONAL CENTER for
YOUTH ISSUES

DUPLICATION AND COPYRIGHT

NCYI titles may be purchased in bulk at special discounts for educational, business, fundraising, or promotional use. For more information, please email sales@ncyi.org.

P.O. Box 22185 • Chattanooga, TN 37422-2185
423-899-5714 • 866-318-6294 • fax: 423-899-4547
www.ncyi.org

ISBN: 9781953945952
E-book ISBN: 9781953945969
Library of Congress Control Number: 2024942657
© 2024 National Center for Youth Issues, Chattanooga, TN
All rights reserved.

Written by: Allison Edwards
Published by National Center for Youth Issues
Printed in the U.S.A.
August 2024

CONTENTS

See page 108 for information about Downloadable Resources.

INTRODUCTION

The first eighteen years of life. That's our window.

As adults, 95 percent of the time we have with children is in the first eighteen years. Those years are our primary opportunity to ensure kids have positive role models and help them learn how to interact and socialize. Ultimately, those years are the time we have to enable children to become functioning adults and citizens of the world who are resilient and able to bounce back when life inevitably tries to knock them down. But the years go by fast. We need to cherish these days with children to prepare them for the road ahead.

It's easy to do the opposite and try to prepare the road for the child. As caregivers, we can go to great lengths to get them into the right type of schools, signed up for the right types of activities, and surrounded by the right types of people. As educators, we can extend deadlines, offer support after the day ends, and stretch ourselves so our students won't have to stretch as much. As counselors, we can stay late, schedule extra sessions, and make accommodations so that kids will carry a lighter load. While these attempts may ease the burden in the short term, kids who do not learn how to struggle in childhood will not know how to manage struggle as adults.

In this book, I will outline a path to prepare children emotionally for the road ahead. This path will teach children to identify feelings, manage behaviors, and build emotional muscles while they are still in our homes and schools—before they face the challenges of the world on their own. This path requires a "wraparound" approach that includes counselors, educators, and parents so that this training takes place in all areas of their lives. Classroom teachers and counselors, with the support of parents, can teach kids the steps to emotion regulation. Along the way, adults will learn how to regulate their own emotions so they can model successful emotion management.

This training can start very early. Children can learn about feelings in Pre-K so that, by the time they enter kindergarten, they possess effective coping strategies to manage them. Our middle schoolers will be able to say, *"I feel angry when you don't let me use my iPad,"* instead of *"Let me have it! It's not fair!"* Adults will be able to identify the feelings they have while in conflict with a child and use coping strategies to manage them. A teacher will be able to say, *"I feel angry at a 7 when James doesn't turn in his notebook. I am going to walk away and take three breaths before I address this issue with him."* A counselor will be able to teach the four steps of emotion regulation to every student who enters their office.

MY "WHY" FOR WRITING THIS BOOK

In the spring of 2023, a school shooting took place at Covenant School in Nashville—just two miles from my office. Having my own two kids in schools nearby and counseling children who were either at the school during the shooting or knew kids who attended the school, I found there weren't enough emotional muscles to be prepared for such an event.

Following the shooting, I met with kids who devised plans to avoid being shot, such as climbing in the ceiling tiles or not allowing themselves to drink water during the school day to avoid going to the bathroom. One child said, *"Since I play sports after school, I'll allow myself to start drinking water at 1:30 so I won't have to use the bathroom at school."*

Another child shared, *"Going to the bathroom is when you'll get shot."*

Another student, just weeks after the shooting had a panic attack during a fire drill. *"I thought, 'This is it,'"* she said, recalling the event.

What's even more alarming are the kids I spoke to who were relatively unfazed by the incident. One teen said, *"I've grown up in the Newtown era."* She went on, *"If twenty six-year-olds can be killed in five minutes at a school, it's always a possibility for me."*

Another child said, *"Every time I hear a loud noise, I jump. Another student's water bottle fell off the top of their desk and I nearly jumped out of my seat. The thing is, other kids jumped too. Even the teacher. We're all afraid. So now we have a new rule that no metal water bottles are allowed in class."* I shared how sad I was to hear this, and she replied, *"That's just our reality."*

When I think back to my own childhood and the anxiety I felt, I can't imagine adding school violence to my plate. I can't imagine sitting in a classroom terrified of a fire drill or the sound of a water bottle falling off a desk, but this is what today's kids feel they have to do. One art teacher I met shared that her colleagues had quietly devised a plan to go behind a hidden door in the school if a school shooter came in. During a school shooter drill, her colleagues thought it was real and took off to the hidden door. It took an hour to find them. *"I guess they were just going to leave me,"* the art teacher said. *"Guess I know where I stand with them."*

I finished this book in Portugal, where I spent six weeks with my family. After the school shooting, I needed a professional sabbatical to step away from my practice and take a breath. The grief I have felt for children and the violence placed on them is palpable. My kids were in a summer program and on a bulletin board, were words written in bold, **Children's Rights.** I am going to begin this book with their words to demonstrate what they value, and what matters to them. After all, they will be our future and their voices will be what matters   most.

I have the right to have a house.

I have the right to be protected.

I have the right to play.

I have the right to be taken care of.

I have the right to have someone listen to me.

I have the right to feel loved.

Wishing all of you love as you parent, educate, and counsel the future of this world. In this book, I hope you learn not only how to build emotional muscles in children, but also to value them, respect them, and know they are the lights, leading us on to better things. As you journey, help the kids, and help yourself. We can never outgrow emotional regulation.

My hope is that readers of this book will join me in changing the paradigms of how we address mental health in children. We will help children identify feelings beneath behaviors and learn how to manage them. We will watch children build emotional muscles and begin facing challenges on their own. And finally, we will gain relief in knowing we have prepared kids well for the road ahead. Let's get started.

Allison

CHAPTER ONE

WHY FEELINGS MATTER

This book is about the management of feelings, but before we discuss how to manage them, it's important to understand why they matter so much. Our feelings are the driving force in our life experience. They are what help us understand the world around us, alert us to danger, nudge us to make decisions or say things we need to say. Feelings themselves are beautiful and make us unique. But feelings are not so beautiful when they are big, overwhelming, and keep us from doing things we need to do or really care about. This stark contrast between the beauty of feelings and the fear of them is what makes feelings so bittersweet.

So, what are feelings?

According to the American Psychological Association, a feeling is "a self-contained phenomenal experience:" and feelings are "subjective, evaluative, and independent of the sensations, thoughts, or images evoking them."[1] What this means in lay terms is that feelings are within yourself and are your interpretations of the world. Feelings are not experienced in the same way by any two people, and they are not a common, collective experience. Because they are our interpretations of what is happening outside of us, they are often misunderstood by others around us.

Example: Two Friends Go to a Popular Music Event

- **Friend One:** Feelings of excitement, joy, happiness
- **Friend Two:** Feelings of fear, frustration, sadness

The two friends were at the same event, but both had very different feelings about the event. Friend One had positive feelings, but Friend Two heard a song that made her think about a past relationship and therefore felt negative feelings. Neither friend is wrong in their feelings, but Friend One is confused as to why Friend Two isn't enjoying herself.

This scenario is common in our interactions with kids. We plan vacations, make special arrangements, and go to a lot of effort to make a fun lesson plan or school event for a child, and then they experience negative feelings. The gap between our *expectations* about their feelings and their actual feelings creates a conflict that often leads to frustration and confusion. When we expect children to have positive feelings and they exhibit negative ones, we want to try to make them feel differently.

Example: Student Wins an Award

You are a counselor, and a child just received an award in school. You are meeting with the child, and they share disappointment. Your natural inclination may be to help them see the good in the situation and be proud of themselves. Instead, it's better to acknowledge their feeling and explore their experience of the award. You can say, *"It sounds like you're disappointed that you received the award. Let's talk about why that is the case for you."*

This reframe becomes harder when you are the one who is directly involved in creating a positive experience for a child.

Example: Student Turns an Assignment in Late

You are a teacher and have allowed a student to turn an assignment in late. You are expecting the child to be grateful for this accommodation and, even though it will be more work for you, you are willing to do it because you care about the student. Instead of being grateful, the child shows frustration in having to turn the assignment in at all.

It's hard to acknowledge and accept this frustration, but it's still better to acknowledge the frustration and, more importantly, not become frustrated yourself.

It's also hard to see a child exhibit negative emotions when others around them seem happy and excited, especially when you are the parent. As parents, we often take our child's feelings personally. If our child is sad or unhappy, we feel like we are the ones to blame and we are the ones who need to fix the problem. This is not the case. Children's feelings are their own and are separate from us. We can help them learn to manage their feelings but feelings, at their core, are experienced separately from others.

Example: Your Child Often Has a Negative Attitude

You are a parent of a child who is routinely feeling negatively. Things never seem good enough and, on a beautiful Saturday morning, your child wakes up irritable and angry. You have made their favorite breakfast, have a day full of fun activities planned, and all you hear from them is negativity.

It would be easy to try to talk the child out of their feelings but in doing so you are devaluing their experience. It's better to accept their feelings and move on with the day. It's also important, in this situation, not to change plans or take away activities due to the negativity. This will only reinforce negativity. A good rule of thumb when kids, or anyone for that matter, experience feelings different from those you expect is to remember:

1. **Everyone is entitled to their own feelings.**
2. **Don't take it personally.**

This will take the pressure off you, as the adult, to make a child happy. It will also show the child that you value their feelings and perceptions about those experiences.

THE DIFFERENCE BETWEEN FEELINGS AND EMOTIONS

The words "feelings" and "emotions" are often used interchangeably, but there are key differences between the two. Emotions are chemical reactions in the body, whereas feelings are the responses to those reactions. Let's look at the differences below:

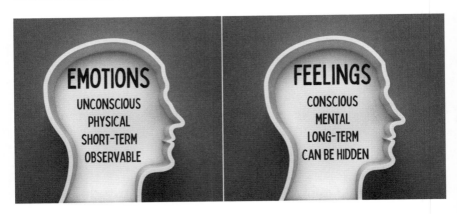

In my book, *Flooded*,[2] I talk about the emotional responses to triggering events that stem from the amygdala. The book was focused on the body and how to reset the brain using the senses, not thought. In this book, we are focusing on feelings, or what happens *after* the body's response. Both are important to understand as they make up the picture of mental health.

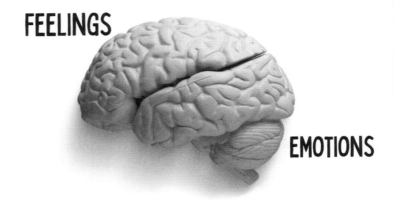

As you can see from the above image, *emotion* comes from the base of the brain or primal brain. The primal brain does not allow for reasoning or thought. It is automatic and is only functioning to survive. *Feeling* is what occurs as the emotion rises from the primal brain to the top brain, where it can be filtered through the lens of thought.

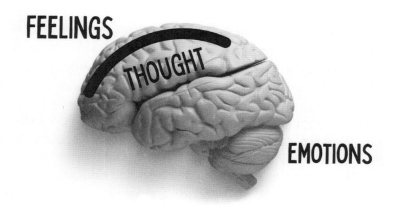

Because of this key factor—thought—we can work with feelings much more than we can with emotions. We can adjust thoughts to help feelings become more manageable. **This is a powerful component of emotion regulation.**

Psychology and counseling are geared toward thoughts and feelings, specifically how to change thoughts to help feelings become more manageable. Changing thoughts is the foundation of Cognitive Behavioral Therapy and is a powerful tool to improve mental health. The awareness of feelings coupled with the ability to change negative thoughts is a powerful combination that helps kids manage difficult emotions.

I also want to mention that while emotions are automatic and come regardless of environment, beliefs, or upbringing, feelings are highly dependent on these factors. Because thoughts affect feelings and thoughts are learned in belief systems, our beliefs about feelings and their expression will affect how we react to them. From the chart shared earlier in this section, we learned feelings can be hidden. Hiding feelings is often a behavior learned in childhood.

HOW OUR CHILDHOOD AFFECTS OUR CURRENT BELIEFS AND FEELINGS

Many of us grew up in environments where feelings weren't valued. We were taught to be tough and strong and to "buck up" when things got hard. Our parents, caregivers and educators were often taught the same approach in their childhoods. Consequently, generations of ignoring and suppressing feelings have led our current generation of educators, parents, and counselors to be unsure of what to do with the expression of emotions, especially negative ones. Many who grew up in a "buck up" mentality have continued the same approach in parenting and education. They are tough on students and their own kids and employ the same "buck up" mentality with themselves.

Others have taken the opposite approach and have become very invested in children having positive feelings. They make accommodations, allow kids to get out of hard tasks and make great effort to keep kids emotionally comfortable. I call this the "bubble wrap" approach. In the "bubble wrap" approach, there is a fear of kids struggling and when kids do hit an emotional bump, the trigger is often removed so kids don't have to feel the negative effects. While there is short-term emotional relief in this approach, the long-term consequences is that kids can't develop resilience.

While both the "buck up" and "bubble wrap" approaches are rooted in good intentions, they both fail to help kids acknowledge emotions *and* do hard things. The "buck up" approach ignores emotions. The "bubble wrap" approach removes hard things. Neither approach is ideal. Instead, I recommend a "scaffolding approach" which supports kids emotionally in doing hard things.

Let's look at the differences in the messages below:

BUCK UP	BUBBLE WRAP	SCAFFOLDING
Get over it.	I'll take care of it.	You can do it.
It's not a big deal.	It may be too hard.	I believe in you.
Stop crying.	You don't have to go.	How can I support you?

The scaffolding approach gives kids the support they need to overcome the challenges of childhood. As children walk through life, they are supported by caring educators, counselors, and parents. They are still expected to do hard things, but the messages they hear from adults include three components:

1. **Empathy and recognition of feelings**
2. **Maintaining boundaries**
3. **Teaching a coping strategy and/or making a plan**

The scaffolding approach provides the ability for kids to do hard things, and build confidence, self-esteem, and self-worth while still under the roofs of our homes and schools—well within our primary window of contact. As we move through this book, we will see how this approach will help kids get to where they need to be emotionally before heading out into the world.

AT HOME
The Scaffolding Approach

Child: *"I don't want to go to the piano recital!"*

Parent: *"I know you're worried about going but they are expecting you."*

Child: *"It is scary! I really don't want to go."*

Parent: *"Scary things are hard, and I am here to help you. Let's take a walk and reset our brains for a few minutes. Then, we can listen to your favorite song on the car ride there. You can use your headphones to help you calm your brain."*

AT SCHOOL

The Scaffolding Approach

CLASSROOM EXAMPLE

Student: *"I didn't know we had an assignment due today! Can I turn it in tomorrow?"*

Teacher: *"I know you're frustrated that you don't have yours completed but it wouldn't be fair to the other students if I let you turn it in late. Let's come up with a plan for you to turn it in on time for the next deadline."*

COUNSELING EXAMPLE

Student: *"Where were you yesterday? I thought we had an appointment scheduled. I was outside your door waiting on you! Can I see you now?"*

Counselor: *"I know you're angry that I wasn't here for our session yesterday, but I needed to be out of the office unexpectedly. I am heading to a meeting now but if you write down your feelings we can talk about them during our next appointment."*

The scaffolding approach helps kids do hard things with empathy. We never want to keep kids from doing hard things because only through accomplishing hard things repeatedly will they gain the confidence they need to do hard things while managing their feelings.

Now, let's look at the most common childhood feelings and how to teach kids about them.

The Top 20 Feelings Children Experience in Childhood

Surprised	Embarrassed	Silly	Jealous
Excited	Frustrated	Angry	Worried
Happy	Lonely	Proud	Disappointed
Sad	Confused	Shy	Calm
Brave	Confident	Hopeful	Overwhelmed

There are many more feelings, but it's important for children to be able to learn at least these twenty feelings in childhood. When I was a school counselor, I started every classroom lesson by pointing to a row of feeling pictures on the wall saying a feeling, and then asking the class to repeat the feeling. I started this with kindergarten students, many of whom did not know the feelings when the school year started. Within a few weeks, each child would go around the room and be able to name the feeling they were experiencing. Children can learn new things in such a short time because of brain neuroplasticity and the rapid rate of brain growth during childhood.

NEUROPLASTICITY AND FEELINGS

A child's brain is much like an onion. If you slice an onion down the middle, you can see the core and then the layers that surround the core. Birth to age five is the core of the onion and when the most rapid brain development occurs. When neurons fire together, they wire together, and since humans are wired to try repeatedly, neurons fire over and over until a task is completed. Once a baby learns to walk, the neurons are wired together, thus creating neuroplasticity.

As kids begin to grow and develop, layers surround their core. They develop reactions, coping strategies, and ways to manage their feelings. If they don't get support in their early years, many of the coping strategies they develop to manage feelings will be maladaptive. Kids often resort to unhealthy methods to manage their feelings and, if no intervention takes place, they can wind up in very precarious situations as teenagers. Let's look at an example of a child who struggles with worry at a young age and the results of early intervention versus no intervention:

EARLY INTERVENTION

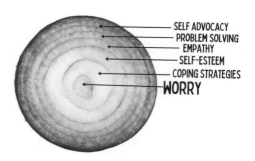

SELF ADVOCACY
PROBLEM SOLVING
EMPATHY
SELF-ESTEEM
COPING STRATEGIES
WORRY

NO INTERVENTION

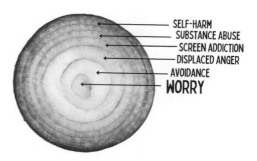

SELF-HARM
SUBSTANCE ABUSE
SCREEN ADDICTION
DISPLACED ANGER
AVOIDANCE
WORRY

The child who received early intervention learned coping strategies and began developing self-esteem, empathy, and, eventually, the ability to self-advocate despite feeling intense worry. The child who received no intervention developed avoidance strategies to manage worry, which turned into addictive behaviors and eventually self-harm. Not all kids who struggle with feelings develop addiction or self-harm but kids who do not get the support they need will inevitably try to manage feelings on their own, without the support of trusting adults.

ROOT FEELINGS

There are twenty important feelings in childhood, but each child will generally have one that will be more important than the others. I call these "root feelings" because they are felt more intensely and more frequently than the others. My root feeling is worry, and I have felt worry more frequently and more intensely than any other feeling since I was a child. Since root feelings are so intense, they often become the driving force in our decisions and, ultimately, our lives. In the image below, you can see life, the road where others are traveling, and then you see a detour.

This detour is created by a root feeling that is not managed. The feeling is so intense that the road seems impossible to travel. Over time, root feelings keep us from living our fullest lives. We miss out on experiences and opportunities because we feel unable to manage the intensity of the root feeling.

Root feelings never really go away. I still feel worry as an adult. What changes is that root feelings become less intense the more we overcome them. We can continue down the road (instead of taking the detour), empowered by learned strategies to manage that root feeling. This does not mean that we won't feel our root feeling on the journey. It just means that we don't let our root feeling keep us from the journey. It comes along with us.

What's so amazing about root feelings is that since they are so intense and so frequent, we can use them to our advantage. I call this a "super skill." Below, we can see how to turn a root feeling into a super skill.

Turning a Root Feeling into a Super Skill

Super skills are abilities that are unique to us, based on our root feeling. Basically, if you turn a root feeling inside out to see the good in it, and use it effectively, it becomes a super skill. I like to describe this to kids by using a geode, as in the image below.

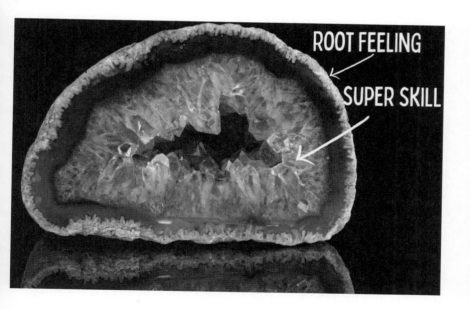

You wouldn't know how beautiful this geode is if you didn't crack it open to see the inside. It's the same with root feelings. On the outside, they are hard and ugly and seem to do nothing but hinder us. But if we look closely and crack them open, we can see the beauty and power that lie within, which help propel us through our lives.

Example: Root Feeling - SAD

Juan is a boy who struggles with sadness. He feels sad more often than other kids and seems to notice the hurt in others and in the world.

Automatic response: avoidance, isolation

Juan tries to avoid his sadness through humor. He tries to make everyone laugh in class but, when he's alone, he hides in his bedroom away from others.

But what if Juan doesn't avoid his sadness and instead learns how to channel it? What if Juan turned his root feeling into a super skill? It would look something like this:

Channeled Response:

Juan starts paying attention to his own sadness and observes the same feeling in others. He notices the sad girl on the playground and even the sadness in his mom when she talks about the divorce from his father. Juan begins drawing other people and using art to help him understand his own sadness and the emotions of others. In high school, he begins to fine-tune his art and receives a scholarship to an art college.

ROOT FEELINGS REFLECTION

The above story is true. I have seen countless kids harness root feelings and turn them into super skills. Now, think about a child you work with or parent and consider these questions:

- **What is one Root Feeling for this child?**
- **What is their Automatic Response?**

- **What could be their Channeled Response?**

Think about what they could be capable of if they channeled their root feeling into a super skill.

Ask yourself what your root feeling is and how (or whether) you are channeling it. Look back through your life and identify your super skill and the purposes it has served. For most of us, our root feeling is what we have tried to run away from, but it is also what has helped us get to where we are.

- **Everyone is entitled to their own feelings.**

- **Emotions are chemical reactions. Feelings are responses to the reactions.**

- **Early intervention is always best.**

- **A root feeling is the feeling you struggle with the most.**

- **A super skill is a root feeling turned inside out.**

KEY POINTS TO REMEMBER

CHAPTER TWO

THE FIVE FEELINGS KIDS NEED TO MANAGE BEFORE AGE 18

Now that we understand feelings, it's important to know which ones matter the most in childhood. If you think of childhood as lasting 18 years, the beginning of the timeline starts at birth and ends when kids become legal adults. Our best opportunity to prepare kids for life is while they are in our homes and schools. After they leave things tend to turn out for the worst if they are not prepared.

BIRTH   1 2 3 4 5 6 7 8 9 10 11 12 13 14 15 16 17   **ADULTHOOD**

0   **OPPORTUNITY**   **18**

In March 2024, *Best Colleges*[3] revealed that 77percent of college students experienced moderate to severe psychological distress. 35 percent of students were diagnosed with anxiety and 27 percent had depression. Even with those high numbers, just 40 percent of students felt their college was doing enough to support their mental health. As many of you remember from your own experience, leaving home is a big adjustment. Without parents nearby and familiar faces of classmates and teachers, life after high school can be scary. But, if we teach kids how to manage their feelings *before* leaving home, things will be much easier for them.

Below are the five most important feelings kids must learn to manage before 18. This does not mean kids won't still struggle with these feelings, but they will know how to cope with them effectively. The five feelings are:

1. **WORRY**
2. **SADNESS**
3. **ANGER**
4. **DISAPPOINTMENT**
5. **LONELINESS**

As we move through this chapter, I will share how to manage each feeling at home and school and then share a coping strategy for each setting. There are additional coping strategies in the Resources section of this book. If you are an educator, counselor, or parent of a young child (or children), you can begin thinking about how you will help kids manage these feelings as we work through this chapter. If you are working with or parenting older children, think about which feelings they might already know how to manage and which ones they need to work on.

FEELING #1: WORRY

We will begin with worry, as anxiety is the most prevalent mental health disorder, affecting forty million adults in the United States.[4] The root feeling of anxiety is worry and most adults identify feeling anxious about their own well-being as well as their children's. Generalized Anxiety Disorder is the most common type of anxiety and is an undercurrent of fear.[5] There are different types of worries on the surface, but those worries will change as life events change.

Here's the way I describe **Generalized Anxiety Disorder:**

You are walking through a tunnel and become hooked by a fear. You remain hooked until become hooked by a stronger fear. You will only be released from each hook when another hook is big enough to grab you away from the last one.

In the image below, you see different hooks that can cause worry in a child. The hooks aren't the problem, it's the mind's continual grabbing of the hooks that is the problem.

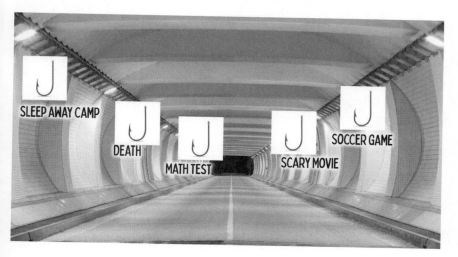

An anxious mind is full of mental energy. Energy can't be stopped, only transferred—so anxious kids don't develop a calm mind as anxiety improves. They still have the same amount of mental energy; it's just that the energy is transferred to something positive rather than negative. See the example below:

A common tool I teach to reduce anxiety is **Change the Channel.** The tool teaches that our brains are like a television, and we have the remote control. We can choose which channel we want to be on. This tool helps kids transfer mental energy instead of trying to stop it. If a child is on the current channel of thought: *"I'm afraid I will mess up at the dance recital,"* they can change it to *"I can't wait to have ice cream after the recital."* It's the same energy but channeled in a positive way.

We will learn the steps to emotional regulation in the next chapter, but when it comes to worry, coping strategies are key. Once a child can identify the root feeling—worry—and can learn strategies to manage it, worry becomes much less debilitating.

Kids will generally share their worry with one parent, in a private space. Kids choose the parent who is either around the most or the parent they feel will listen to them the most. Kids who struggle with worry will often wait until the chosen parent is available and share their worry, usually in the form of a question:

Child: "*Do I have to go to school tomorrow?***"**

If the parent stays on the surface and addresses the question, the child will not make gains in managing the worry.

Most parents will say:

Parent: *"Yes, you have to go to school,"* or *"Let's see how you feel when you wake up."*

Both responses fail to address the undercurrent of fear. A better approach is to say,

Parent: *"I know you're worried about going to school tomorrow. Let's make a 'Power Rock'* [explained in Resources section] *for you to hold in your pocket to help you feel safe."*

This approach helps the child learn to manage the fear with a coping strategy. A child will feel worried about many things throughout their life. If you focus on reducing the fear, you will help the child in the long term. If you only focus on the events, you will stay in the short term, endlessly trying to solve problems for your child—and your child will not learn how to manage fear.

What's important to know about worry is this: **worry is fear based on a future event.** When you're worried, you make up a negative story about a future event and *believe* the story. An example is, *"I won't have any friends in my class next year."* This story is fiction. There is no way of knowing if you will have friends in your class.

The anxious mind creates the story, and the child believes it. If the parent tries to contradict the story by saying, *"Of course you'll have friends in your class! You know almost every student in the grade,"* the child will not learn to manage the fear that created the story. Your reaction will likely only fuel the worry by trying to rationalize a child's irrational fear.

Look at the image below:

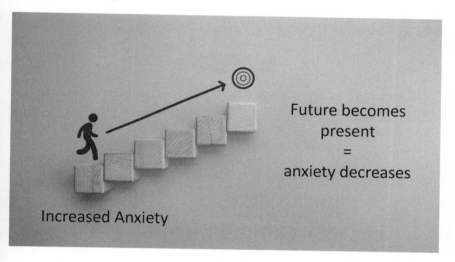

Future becomes present
=
anxiety decreases

Increased Anxiety

Since anxiety is fear of the future, anxiety will increase as you move toward an anxiety-producing event. This is natural. Most kids (and adults) don't want to feel worried, so once worry increases, they try to change course to avoid the situation. *But* if you keep moving toward the anxiety-producing event and walk into it, anxiety will decrease. **The future will become the present, and you will no longer need the story because you will be living the reality.**

If a child can take the steps toward the feared event and continue through it, anxiety will decrease, and confidence will skyrocket. Simply put, **there is no better way to increase confidence in an anxious child than by helping them walk toward and through their most feared experiences.** Below is one of my favorite strategies to help children face their fears.

COPING STRATEGY

FICTION OR FACT?

WHAT YOU NEED:

Fiction or Fact? Worksheet (or a piece of paper) and a pencil

HOW IT WORKS:

Ask the child to write down the story they are making up about a future event in the fiction column. Then, ask them to write down the facts about the event. Be there to help them compare the two categories to see the difference between the story in their mind versus the facts. After they write down the fiction followed by fact(s), they can create a new story that includes the facts. Here is an example using the aforementioned story:

FICTION OR FACT? WORKSHEET

DIRECTIONS: In the **Fiction** box, write down the story that you worry will happen. Next, write down the facts about that event in the **Facts** box. Take some time to consider and compare what you wrote down in the **Fiction** and **Fact** boxes. Finally, write down a **New Story** that includes the facts you listed.

FICTION

I won't have any friends in class.

FACT

I have friends in my current class.
I have gone to this school for five years.
I have always made friends in class.

NEW STORY

I am worried about having friends in class next year. I have had friends in class before. Hopefully, I will have them again.

FACTS HELP MY BRAIN RE-WRITE THE STORY!

Growing Up Strong by Allison Edwards
© National Center for Youth Issues   www.ncyi.org

As you can see, the new story doesn't guarantee friends in class. It suggests that there are facts to prove there is a likelihood of having friends.

WHY IT WORKS:

Anxiety is rigid thinking. When stories become fixed in our minds, they keep us from being open to all possibilities. This strategy breaks up the rigidity of worry and allows flexibility in thinking. This flexibility helps anxious kids see that things are not inherently good or bad, wrong or right. There is room in the middle for seemingly bad things to turn out good or scary things to turn out enjoyable. This strategy also works because it gets the story out of the mind and onto paper. When we can see the stories we create in our minds, we gain a clearer picture of how to change them. Sight is the most powerful sense so often seeing our thoughts and our stories about events helps us let go of them.

AT SCHOOL
How to Help Kids Manage Worry

School is a trigger for kids. It requires academic focus, social interactions, rule-following, and high expectations. Some kids thrive in the school environment and seem to have it all together. Many of those kids fall apart once they get home. Other kids show signs of worry in the classroom. The typical signs of worry at school are:

- Inattention
- School Refusal
- Disruptive Behavior
- Avoidance of Being Called On
- Not Turning in Homework
- Avoidance of Group Work
- Psychosomatic Complaints
- Difficulty Dealing with Change

It is often easy for an educator to spot an anxious child. You can tell by their demeanor, how they interact with other students, and how they approach learning. Some anxious kids can manage anxiety and stay afloat in the school environment. Other kids are so debilitated that their anxiety not only affects them but those around them. One of the most intense forms of worry at school can come out as test anxiety, as shown below:

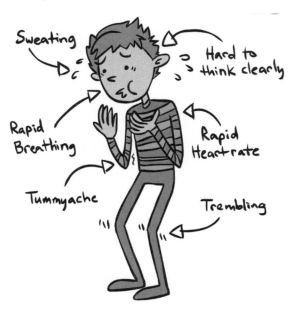

When kids exhibit physical signs of anxiety, it not only affects the anxious student but also others around them. There is a saying that, "anxiety is contagious" and this is true, especially in a testing environment. Whether a student is experiencing test anxiety, social anxiety, or generalized anxiety, the best way to help is to allow them to reset their brains by leaving the classroom. Below is a powerful strategy that gives students the ability to reset their brains and bodies before moving on to a test, interacting with a group, doing a presentation, or simply listening to a lecture.

GIVE AN OUT

WHAT YOU NEED:

Brain Reset Worksheet (or a 5x7 notecard) and a pencil

HOW IT WORKS:

> NAME:_____
>
> ## BRAIN RESET: 5 SENSES IN 5 MINUTES
>
> Something I can SEE: _____
>
> Something I can HEAR:_____
>
> Something I can SMELL: _____
>
> Something I can TASTE: _____
>
> Something I can TOUCH: _____

When a child is anxious at school, they need a plan to reduce that anxiety. **Give an Out** is a tool that helps a child create this plan by knowing how they will reset *before* a triggering event occurs. With a counselor or teacher, the child will fill out the blanks below with how they will reset their brain in five minutes. They can keep the worksheet/card in their desk or backpack and when they feel anxious, they can grab the worksheet/card and leave the classroom to reset their brain.

Just by leaving the classroom, a child can reset nearly all of the senses. They can *see* the hallway, *hear* the sounds of other students, *smell* food in the cafeteria, *taste* a sip of water from the water fountain, and *touch* cool water as they wash their hands in the bathroom. This has worked so well for many kids that they have created their own reset kit that they take to school every day. Some ideal items for a reset kit are below:

1. Lavender oil - smell
2. Picture of family or pet - see
3. Mini Altoid® mints – taste

Rock with a heart drawn on the front – touch Some kids can reset their sense of hearing by the simple act of leaving the classroom. Other kids enjoy whistling to hear something different. Whistling also provides a good distraction, and kids can whistle their favorite songs as a part of the reset process.

WHY IT WORKS:

This strategy empowers kids to manage anxiety in the school setting. Without needing to call a parent, see the school counselor, or leave school, kids can reset all on their own. This strategy also helps kids reset their brains in areas besides school and home. Kids can take their reset pouches to sleepovers, sleep-away camps, and on vacation, enabling them to reset their brains no matter where they are. The ability to reset the brain is a life-long skill that anyone can use, including teachers, counselors, and parents. I even use this tool in my daily work as a counselor. When I feel overwhelmed or worried, I leave my office and take five minutes to walk outside and allow myself to reset the senses. I also use lavender oil in my office, which provides an automatic reset during the workday.

FEELING #2: SADNESS

If you think of anxiety and depression on a continuum, they both have negative thinking in common. Sadness is negative thinking about the past and anxiety is negative thinking about the future.

DEPRESSION   **ANXIETY**

(PAST)   ←——————————————→   **(FUTURE)**

NEGATIVE THINKING

It's normal to feel sad, but when it is prolonged and interferes with daily functioning, it can lead to depression. Kids can fluctuate between anxiety and depression, but what's most important is to know that both anxiety and depression distort the view of reality. When I describe depression, I say it's as if you're wearing contact lenses that make you see things negatively.

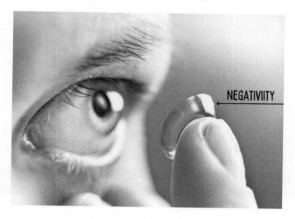

There is a lens of negativity that's so close to your vision you can't see anything else. For example: a child can seemingly have a fabulous day at the park but then come home and say they didn't have any fun. Alternatively, you can see a child at a school event, with lots of fun things to do, withdraw from others and say they want to go back to their classroom. Both scenarios can be confusing as there seems to be no apparent reason why a child would not experience positive feelings. In these cases, the lens of negativity clouds their vision and causes them to find the negative in a seemingly in all positive situations.

Kids who struggle with sadness often make extreme statements such as:

- **I don't have any friends.**
- **I'm stupid.**
- **No one likes me.**
- **You don't love me.**
- **This is the worst day ever.**

While these statements are hard to hear from kids, it's important to not try to convince the child otherwise. Instead, acknowledge the feeling and accept how the child sees the situation. Since sadness is rear-view thinking, kids will often have a hard time letting go of the past. They remember teachers they didn't like, the last-second shot they missed in a basketball game, or the comment they made that hurt someone's feelings. Again, it's not important to counteract these statements but rather to acknowledge the feelings underneath them. As we discussed in the last chapter, the feelings they express are their own and it's important to allow kids to feel them, even if they seem off-base or irrational.

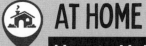

AT HOME
How to Help Kids Manage Sadness

You can take your child to a theme park, watch them have a blast, and when they come home, they say they didn't have fun. You can also watch them looking miserable at a party or event where other kids seem to be enjoying themselves and wonder, *"What's wrong with my child?"* Below is a common scenario:

You take off work, plan a fun day with your child, have one-on-one time, and it goes fabulously. When you get home, your child is pouty, and the following interaction occurs:

Child: *"You never spend time with me."*

Parent: *"I took the whole day off to spend time with you!"*

In the above situation, the parent is frustrated because the child didn't acknowledge the effort and quality time the parent spent with them. In these cases, it's tempting to try to convince your child that their view is not accurate—but that will not be useful. They are seeing the world through a lens of negativity, so you will not be able to convince them otherwise. It would be better to respond in the following way:

Child: *"You never spend time with me."*

Parent: *"I'm sorry you're feeling sad about our time spent together."*

In the above scenario, the parent acknowledges the child's feeling and leaves it at that. There is no need to explain how much effort the parent made to take off work, make plans for the day, etc. If you try and explain that to a child, you will only exacerbate the negativity.

Some parents bend over backward to help their children feel less sad. They spend tons of energy planning events and social interactions to make their child happy, and when those events and interactions don't work, parents get even more frustrated. If your child struggles with sadness, it's important not to overcompensate for the sadness but to acknowledge moments of joy—in the moment—so a child can begin to acknowledge them as well.

Because positivity does not come naturally to a child who struggles with sadness, there needs to be an outside perspective that can help them see the good. Pointing out the good will not work if your child is stuck in a rut of negativity. But when your child seems to be having fun, seize the moment—which brings us to our next strategy.

COPING STRATEGY

GOOD THINGS JAR

WHAT YOU NEED:

Clay and beads

HOW IT WORKS:

Roll a small lump of clay into a ball. Press your thumbs down in the middle of the ball, almost to the bottom, and then pinch around the sides. This makes a pinch pot—a simple way to make a small jar. Your child can make the jar (or you can) but what's important is to avoid adding stress to the strategy. It should be fun! Then explain to your child that you are making a jar of good things. Take a bead and say, *"What is something good that happened today?"* When your child tells you something good, add the bead to the jar. Your child can keep adding beads as long as they share one good thing that has happened for each bead.

Kids love adding beads to the jar. The incentive of having more beads will allow them to think about the good things in their life. Once kids start to see the good things, it breaks the cycle of only seeing the bad. This is a great strategy to have as a bedtime routine. As kids reflect on their day, they can see the positive as they end the day and head off to sleep.

If you have an older child, you can do this strategy verbally. In the evening, just before bed, you can ask your child how their day went and talk about the good things that happened. If your child is in a negative mood, you don't want to press this strategy. Instead, let them share their negative view and say, *"I hope some good things happen tomorrow."* A stream of sadness can be broken up with only a few positive experiences.

AT SCHOOL
How to Help Kids Manage Sadness

Sadness comes out in a variety of ways in school. Educators spend more time with kids than their parents and are often the first to notice sadness in a child. Below are some signs of sadness at school:

- seeming tired, lacking energy, giving up easily
- putting little effort into schoolwork
- having trouble concentrating in class
- failing to turn in work, getting lower grades
- lacking a sense of enjoyment
- withdrawing from friends or activities
- missing school days, or frequently late

If you notice these signs in students, try and make a connection with them. Instead of focusing on their academics, ask questions about how they are doing overall. The following questions are good ways to begin a conversation:

- *"How are you? You seem to be down lately."*
- *"You doing ok?"*
- *"I'm worried about you."*
- *"I'm here if you need to talk."*

Some kids feel closer to their teachers than they do to their parents and will open up when given the chance. Educators are a great resource for kids, especially educators who are safe and relatable. If a child expresses a great deal of struggle, it's best to share that information with parents and school mental health supports such as counselors, social workers, and psychotherapists. The Academy of Pediatrics reported that 75 percent of children receive mental health treatment at school, which means school is the primary source of support for children experiencing emotional distress.[6] When working with a child who struggles with sadness at school, it's important to start breaking up the tightly bound belief that life is inherently bad and that things aren't working out. Below is a great strategy to help children acknowledge the positive.

BREAKING IT DOWN

WHAT YOU NEED:

Dominos

HOW IT WORKS:

When a student reports having a bad day, bring out a set of dominos and ask, *"What is the first thing that happened today?"* This could be the first thing that happened when they woke up or the first thing that happened when they arrived at school. When the student responds, set a domino up on its end. Then ask, *"What happened next?"* and place another domino next to it. Keep this sequence up until the child has reported the events leading up to the moment you are sitting with them. You may have four or five dominos in a line or there may be many more. What's important is that they are in a straight line.

Ask, *"What if I pushed the end of the dominos down?"* and discuss how all the dominos will fall into a pile, and it would be hard to see which dominos represented each event.

Then ask the child to pull out the dominos that represent the good things that happened today. For example, a good thing might be: *"talked to my friend at lunch,"* or *"got a good grade on a math test."* Talk about why these were good things and how often good things happen. Then, ask them to set the dominos of good things in a line next to the bad things and compare them. Discuss how both good and bad things happened, but also how sometimes it can seem like only bad things happened when you think of a day as a whole. As the child compares the two, they can see the ups and downs of a day and acknowledge that both good and bad things happened.

WHY IT WORKS:

This strategy works because it helps kids see the ups and downs of a given day in a concrete way. They have a visual of each segment of the day rather than a mental interpretation that the day was all bad. It also works because it doesn't convince kids to see things differently. Instead of trying to help them see the good, you are asking them to recount the events of their day and share how they felt. They are the ones who determine whether an event was positive. Sadness is like a blanket covering everything up into one emotion. This strategy breaks up the day, allowing children to become aware of the parts, instead of the whole, enabling them to see the parts that were positive.

FEELING #3: ANGER

Anger is one of the most difficult feelings to manage. Anger causes a variety of issues for adults, including health problems (high blood pressure, headaches, anxiety), low self-esteem, troubles with relationships, diminished well-being, and less productivity at work, so it's very important that kids learn to manage anger before reaching adulthood. Let's begin with understanding what anger is: Anger is considered a secondary feeling, which means it is fueled by other feelings.[7] Let's look at the anger iceberg below:

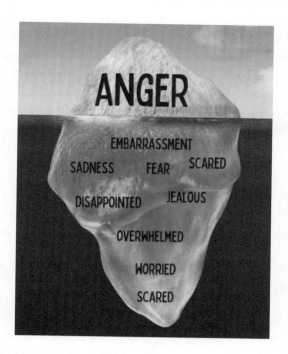

You can see there are many feelings underneath the surface that can emerge as anger. The reason kids don't acknowledge the feeling underneath the anger is either 1) they are unaware of the feeling, or 2) anger is the more accepted way of expressing feelings in their environment. Many kids feel they must be strong and not show any sign of weakness. This message may be modeled in the home environment, at school, or in peer groups. Kids whose parents express anger by yelling or saying hurtful things will learn to do the same. Kids on athletic teams may be taught to be aggressive and show no fear. In peer groups, it's often more accepted to say mean things or retaliate when hurt by a peer than to admit the hurt.

As adults, it's important for us to do two things to help children manage anger:

1. Acknowledge the feelings underneath anger.
2. Set boundaries to help manage anger in healthy ways.

Acknowledge the Feelings Underneath Anger

Many kids don't know what they are feeling. Their behavior comes out as anger but, beneath the surface, there is a root feeling they are unaware of. As adults, we can help them identify the feeling and acknowledge it. This helps kids understand their inner world and what is driving their anger.

Example:

> **Child:** *"I want to go to the baseball game tonight! Why can't I go? It's not fair. You never take me anywhere!"*
>
> **Parent:** *"I know you're <u>disappointed</u> we can't go to the game tonight."*

This response acknowledges the child's disappointment and brings awareness to the feeling. Disappointment isn't a feeling most children identify immediately but it is a very critical feeling to manage. The child may have no idea they were disappointed, but this statement brings awareness and gives their behavior context. Instead of simply getting in trouble for throwing a fit when they didn't get to go to the baseball game, they will learn they were disappointed, and this awareness will help them learn about their inner world. When kids can recognize and deal with their primary feeling (in this case, disappointment) behind the secondary emotion (anger), they become better able to manage the anger itself.

Setting Boundaries to Help Kids Manage Anger

It's often not enough to acknowledge the feeling when it comes to anger. It's also important to set boundaries so kids don't make choices that hurt themselves and others. In interacting with kids who exhibit anger in an unhealthy way, I recommend using the **ACT Method**. The ACT Method is best used when a child becomes physical (hitting, kicking, pushing) or is yelling at others. Outlined below are the steps to the ACT Method:

1. **Acknowledge** the Feeling — *"I see that you're angry."*
2. **Communicate** the Limit — *"But I am not for hitting."*
3. **Target** an Alternative — *"You can hit this pillow if you like."*

This way of communicating helps defuse anger and gives kids an alternative. In this interaction, you are not trying to find the root feeling. Instead, you are helping a child make a better choice. You also are not targeting the child or saying, *"Don't do that,"* or *"Stop that."* You are setting a boundary without placing blame. You are also breaking the behavior pattern by giving a different response. I have used this method time and again in my office and have watched children who are getting ready to throw sand or break a toy stop in their tracks because my response was so different from the response they are used to.

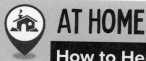

AT HOME

How to Help Kids Manage Anger

Home is the most common place for anger to come out because home is a safe place. Kids who bottle up feelings all day will often come home and say something mean to their parents or hit their siblings as a way to release their feelings. As a parent, you may have no idea what triggered the feeling, but it's important to *not* do two things:

1. Respond with anger
2. Single your child out for the inappropriate behavior

For example, if your child hits their sibling, instead of saying, *"Don't hit your brother,"* say *"In our family, we don't hit."* The second statement doesn't single your child out but helps them understand the family rules. You can still give a consequence to address the behavior, but you are letting your child know that everyone in the family is expected to follow the house rules.

Kids who express anger at home tend to get in trouble often. This creates a feeling of being a "bad kid" and this belief about oneself is harmful and can lead to shame and low self-worth. It's important to help kids who struggle to manage anger see themselves as separate from their feeling or behavior. For example, saying, *"You are a wonderful child. You just made a poor choice"* or, *"It's okay to feel angry. I feel angry sometimes, too,"* normalizes anger and helps kids see they are not bad or wrong for feeling it.

COPING STRATEGY

RESET TIME

WHAT YOU NEED:

A quiet place and whatever the child needs for their activity

HOW IT WORKS:

When your child comes home from school, set aside time for them to have fifteen minutes to decompress. Before starting homework or playing outside with siblings, find a space for your child to be alone and do a desired activity, such as playing with Legos, reading a favorite book, drawing, listening to music, etc. Siblings may want to be a part of reset time, but I would encourage you to make this time independent of others.

WHY IT WORKS:

When kids are full of feelings, a reset allows time to release them by doing things they enjoy. Many kids need time after school or a taxing event to decompress. Reset time is a perfect way to transition from a tiring event to the evening. After a child has reset, the chances of them having a good evening are far better. You can teach your child to take a reset whenever they feel overwhelmed. This is an important step in learning how to manage feelings on their own.

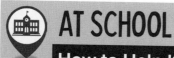

AT SCHOOL

How to Help Kids Manage Anger

Kids who express anger at school also tend to get in trouble or develop negative self-esteem as a result. Anger can come out in different ways at school, but the most common reactions are:

- emotional outbursts
- temper tantrums
- yelling
- lashing out
- hitting

A common strategy in education is to quell the anger to stop the behavior. This includes taking away privileges (like recess), giving verbal reprimands, and sending kids to another room or an administrator's office. This approach is sometimes necessary to keep the classroom environment safe and calm for the other students. There are other times when a student does not need the intervention of a teacher. They may be able to calm down on their own if they are able to shift their mind away from the anger to something concrete and non-triggering. A great strategy to accomplish this is called **What I See. What I Hear.**

COPING STRATEGY

WHAT I SEE, WHAT I HEAR

WHAT YOU NEED:

What You See, What You Hear Worksheet (or a notecard or piece of paper)

HOW IT WORKS:

Teach a student to look around the room and find five objects they see, five colors they see, and five things they hear. Then, they fill in the blanks and share it with a teacher or school counselor. They can also keep it to themselves. If they don't have the worksheet available, they can write the same columns on a sheet of paper or on a notecard.

WHAT YOU SEE, WHAT YOU HEAR WORKSHEET

5 OBJECTS I See	5 COLORS I See	5 SOUNDS I Hear
1.	1.	1.
2.	2.	2.
3.	3.	3.
4.	4.	4.
5.	5.	5.

GROWING UP STRONG

Anger can be intense and take all the mental energy in the brain. If you stay focused on the trigger, anger will continue to increase. If you shift the mind to focus on something else, the anger will defuse, and the mind will be able to regulate again. This strategy is not only useful in a classroom but can be used anywhere a child goes.

Children who struggle with anger are often misunderstood. I worked with a child many years ago who shared that he saw himself as a monster because that's how he behaved. Because anger is intense and quick, it's hard for kids to manage. If they learn how to catch it before it comes out in a harmful or inappropriate way, they can build confidence in knowing they can control their feelings, rather than allow their feelings to control them.

FEELING #4: DISAPPOINTMENT

No one wants to see a child feel disappointed. We want kids to feel successful and happy and to have their needs met. Yet, disappointment is an important feeling to manage as life is filled with disappointments. We don't always get what we want, and things aren't always what they seem. We want kids to feel disappointment in childhood so we can help them manage it while they are in our homes and schools. Kids will feel disappointed for a variety of reasons but some of the most common are:

- being cut from a sports team
- not doing well on a test
- losing a game
- not getting to do something they thought they were going to do
- being left out of a friend group

There can be other disappointments, but what matters most is to help kids experience disappointment and manage it effectively rather than run away from it. Some kids will avoid getting their hopes up because feeling disappointed is just too hard. They will not challenge themselves to do something new or out of their comfort zone so they won't have to face the uncomfortable feeling. If we don't challenge kids to face disappointment, their worlds will become very small. They will only do the sports they are good at, take the classes they know they can ace, only go to social events where they know they'll have friends, etc. While these decisions feel safe in the short term, kids will miss out on wonderful opportunities and experiences that will help them have a fuller life.

As adults, it's important to manage our own feelings when we see children feeling disappointed. It's easy to support a child in doing something we know they'll be good at, but harder to watch them struggle and feel unsuccessful. It's our job to encourage them to try difficult things anyway. The process of going through the challenging experience is what will help them get through other challenging experiences. Over time, disappointments will fade but the strength kids gain from them will remain.

AT HOME
How to Help Kids Manage Disappointment

Many kids act like they aren't bothered by disappointment in public. They seem like they don't care in front of their peers, coaches, and teachers, then come home and fall apart. As parents, we can be there to pick up the pieces when our children are devastated by a disappointing event. The world outside may never know how hard it really was for our child to suffer the disappointment, but we will, and we can be there to support them through it.

As parents, we may respond to their disappointment with a philosophical approach. We may say things like:

- *"It will all work out in the end."*
- *"Everything happens for a reason."*
- *"Someday it will all make sense."*

While these things may be true, they are not useful in the moment. They often make children's disappointment feel minimized, as though their feelings are themselves wrong. A better approach is to acknowledge the feeling and say something like:

- *"I'm so sorry it didn't work out."*
- *"I'm proud of you for trying something new."*
- *"I know you're disappointed. How can I support you?"*

These statements are much more useful because they meet the child where they are and provide empathy and support.

One of the most common mistakes we can make as parents is not validating the child's experience. For example, when a teenager goes through a romantic break-up, some parents may say, *"It's just a high school relationship. It wasn't going to last,"* but that doesn't address the child's feelings or acknowledge the validity of the emotional pain. For anyone who has suffered a high school break-up, the pain was real no matter how old we were at the time. It's useful to remember our own disappointments as children to help us empathize with our own kids.

SOOTHING SPA

WHAT YOU NEED:

Bathtub, bath salts or bubbles, candles, soft music, etc.

HOW IT WORKS:

Explain to your child that when we feel disappointed, it's good to take care of ourselves. Taking a bath is a good way to soothe our bodies and our minds. Help your child set up their soothing spa by filling the bathtub full of warm water. Add salts or bubble baths, light candles, and turn on soft music. You can also dim the lights to help your child feel more relaxed. Set a timer for twenty minutes or let your child stay in the bath as long as desired.

WHY IT WORKS:

Taking a bath is a great way to reset the brain. It calms the senses and helps a child relax. Setting up a soothing spa helps the child feel validated and important. By helping kids learn to take care of themselves, we teach them how to self-soothe. Many kids I work with will set up a soothing spa on Friday evening, after a long week at school, to reward themselves for their hard work. As kids get older, they can set up a soothing spa on their own, whenever they need to be rejuvenated or show themselves some extra love and care.

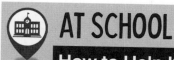

AT SCHOOL

How to Help Kids Manage Disappointment

Educators see disappointment in their students daily. On any given day, an educator will hand back a test and students will be disappointed with their grade. Educators are aware of the kids who struggle academically and can't seem to make progress as quickly as other students. Academics aren't the only area of disappointment among students. Some students have trouble connecting with peers and find ways to avoid being in unstructured social situations. These kids often want to eat lunch in their classroom or the library to avoid the disappointment of not having friends.

It's important to create a safe space as an educator, but there is a fine line between being sensitive to a student's disappointment and accommodating a student's needs so they don't have to feel the feeling. For example:

- Should you let a student turn work in late?
- Should you let a child eat lunch in your classroom?
- Should you offer extra credit to make up for a low test grade?

These are the dilemmas that educators face daily. They are not easy dilemmas to solve but a good rule of thumb is this:

Ask yourself, am I helping or hurting the student in the long term?

For example, if you allow a student to consistently turn work in late, you can't be sure the next teacher will be so lenient. Your accommodation to help a student may only hurt them later as they won't learn the valuable lesson of consequences for missing the deadline. The earlier a student learns about time management, the more successful their academic path will be. The same goes for allowing a student to have extra credit to make up for a low test grade. You may offer this allowance in a special situation (a family member died, an illness occurred, an extracurricular interfered with the test) but if you offer it often, a student will begin to believe the rules don't apply to them.

COPING STRATEGY

50/50

WHAT YOU NEED:

Time for a brief meeting with the student

HOW IT WORKS:

Arrange a meeting with the student and explain that you are going to give 50 percent effort to help the student, but they are going to have to give 50 percent effort as well. For example, if a student received a low grade on a test, you are going to give your 50 percent by allowing them to take the test again this once, but you won't be able to do that next time. The next time will be their 50 percent of having to accept the results. The same would go for a student who turns work in late. You will give 50 percent by letting them turn it in the next day, but they will have to give 50 percent by completing the entire assignment on the given night.

WHY IT WORKS:

Being a good educator means understanding the needs of your students. Every student needs something different and with the 50/50 approach you are giving, but also holding the student accountable. You are not only doing your part but asking them to do theirs. This will help them learn to be accountable while providing the scaffolding to help them learn how to be successful.

FEELING #5: LONELINESS

Some kids like to be alone. They spend time playing or reading alone in their rooms and seem completely happy. Other kids want someone to always be with them. Many introverted kids prefer to do things alone and extroverted kids want to do things with others. This is not what I'm referring to when I describe loneliness. The feeling of loneliness I am referring to is feeling unwanted, disconnected, or that no one understands you. You can have a thriving social life but still feel like no one really gets you. This feeling of being on the outside of the norm causes many kids to struggle internally. Researchers suggest that loneliness is associated with social isolation, poor social skills, introversion, and depression.[8]

There are many causes of loneliness, including having a learning difference, a unique interest that others around you don't share, an emotional struggle such as anxiety or depression, or a gender or sexuality difference that people around you don't support. These differences create stress in kids, and while some kids crave true connection with others, their feeling of being different often keeps them from doing so. Some kids have chronic feelings of loneliness and resort to finding friends online whom they feel "get" them. While it's ok to connect with others online, having friends they can see face-to-face each day is going to help with loneliness more than logging on to a screen.

AT HOME
How to Help Kids with Loneliness

Some kids will keep their loneliness to themselves. They won't tell parents they feel disconnected, empty, or alone. Instead, they withdraw farther and farther inward and, in these cases, loneliness becomes a heavy cloud that hovers over their daily lives. As parents, it's important to have an openness to whatever your child is interested in, who they are, and what they believe. When kids feel their ideas and beliefs don't align with their parents, they will go inward and find connections with others outside the home who will allow them to be who they really are. As parents, loving them unconditionally, without a need to change your child, will allow them to feel connected at home. Feeling connection at home is the foundation for feeling connected to the outside world.

I have counseled many kids over the years who did not have a strong connection with their parents. They felt their parents did not accept who they were or their desire to want something different for their lives. They longed for the time they would be away at college and be their authentic selves. While a change in location and the freedom to connect with others who are similar may help, it will not immediately heal the core feeling of loneliness. The desire to connect with your family of origin is deeply rooted, and the damage that results from the lack of such connection takes many years to heal. As a parent, work toward strengthening your connection to your child so they can feel a strong connection while in your home.

NO-TALK NOTEBOOK

WHAT YOU NEED:

Spiral Notebook

HOW IT WORKS:

Explain to your child that the notebook is to be shared between your child and yourself. They can write anything they want to share with you and there is only one rule: **You can't talk about it.** Your child will write a note to you and leave the notebook in your bedroom. After you read what your child wrote, you can write back. You can ask questions in the note you write back, but you cannot ask them directly to your child. When you see your child in the day-to-day, no matter what they share, you are not allowed to address it with them.

WHY IT WORKS:

This strategy creates a safe space for you and your child to connect. I have worked with parents for many years who have said the No-Talk Notebook is how they found out their child was struggling with depression, having friendship issues, feeling low on confidence, or worried about their future. Without it, those parents would have had no idea. If you have a child who is struggling emotionally but not sharing why, I recommend you start a No-Talk Notebook and allow your child the space they need to have a safe connection and outlet.

AT SCHOOL

How to Help Kids with Loneliness

Loneliness can emerge in different forms at school. Some kids spend lunchtime with their heads tucked behind a book while their peers talk and laugh with one another. Other kids float from friend group to friend group, not getting too close to any one person. Other kids will befriend teachers and other adults in the building to avoid connecting with peers. Being able to connect with peers is a very important part of development. Finding connection and feeling like you are accepted is something every kid truly desires...and deserves.

There are several ways to promote connection with peers, and, as an educator, you are in a prime position to know who the best kids are to make those connections. Educators have a first-hand view of how the kids in their classroom socialize. They can identify students who need connection and safe students who are kind and easy to talk to. Pairing those students together will help a child form a positive connection, and when a child feels connected to just one other student, their feelings of loneliness at school will subside.

PAIRING FOR CONNECTION

WHAT YOU NEED:

An opportunity to group students together

HOW IT WORKS:

Select a student in class who seems disconnected and pair them with a safe, kind student who would be a good fit to make a connection. Allow time for the students to work together on a project one-on-one. A group of more than two students will not be as effective and a disconnected student will likely fall by the wayside. Ask the two students to work together both in and outside of class, allowing them to form a bond. This strategy will be most effective if the project is long-standing, allowing the students to work together for a period of time.

WHY IT WORKS:

Students who experience loneliness at school are hesitant to join friend groups or make efforts to connect. This strategy gives students a concrete task to do together, which lessens anxiety for the lonely student. Working together on a project also gives them something in common, and, from that commonality, more commonalities may be found. Children who feel connected will be more invested in school both academically and socially, thus having a better overall academic experience.

THE TIMELINE

Now that we're aware of the five feelings kids need to manage before age 18, think about a child you teach, counsel, or parent and consider these questions below. (You can also do this exercise using *The Timeline Worksheet* in the Downloadable Resources.)

THE TIMELINE WORKSHEET

Name of child _____

Which of the five feelings does the child currently know how to manage?

- ☐ WORRY
- ☐ SADNESS
- ☐ ANGER
- ☐ DISAPPOINTMENT
- ☐ LONELINESS

What feelings is the child currently unable to manage? _____

How can I teach the child to manage these feelings? What strategies might I use? _____

Circle the age the child is currently. Above the timeline, write the feelings the child is currently able to manage. Then, write the feelings the child needs to learn before age 18.

BIRTH   1 2 3 4 5 6 7 8 9 10 11 12 13 14 15 16 17   ADULTHOOD

0   OPPORTUNITY   18

In the spaces below, you can record additional thoughts, insights, and opportunities that you may have to help a child manage these feelings. _____

Growing Up Strong by Allison Edwards
© National Center for Youth Issues   www.ncyi.org

- Which of the five feelings does the child currently know how to manage?
- What feelings is the child currently unable to manage?
- How can I teach the child to manage these feelings? What strategies might I use?

As I shared at the beginning of this chapter, we have limited time to teach children how to manage what occurs inside of them. This timeline is not intended to put pressure on you but to allow you to make a plan that will accomplish the task before they leave home.

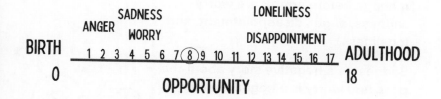

In the example above you see an eight-year-old child (age is circled) who has already learned to manage anger, sadness, and worry. They have not yet managed loneliness and disappointment. The job of the adult in this case is to help the child learn to manage loneliness and disappointment within the next ten years. While that may seem like a long time, there will be other and more intense feelings in adolescence so we never really know what new challenges a child will face. The adult in this situation can provide the child with opportunities to manage these feelings and have strategies to teach along the way.

Now, think about a child you are currently teaching, counseling, or parenting and do this exercise on your own. Consider these questions:

- What is the current age of the child?
- What feelings is the child currently able to manage?
- What are the feelings the child needs to learn before age 18?
- Finally, what are any additional thoughts, insights, and opportunities that you may have to help a child manage these feelings?

- The five feelings children need to manage before age 18 are worry, sadness, anger, disappointment, and loneliness.

- Sadness is a negative story about the past, and worry is a negative story about the future.

- Anger is a secondary feeling and is a result of buried feelings underneath the surface.

- Kids who fear disappointment are often afraid of taking risks so they won't have to feel disappointed.

- Feeling connected at home leads to kids feeling connected to the outside world.

KEY POINTS TO REMEMBER

CHAPTER THREE

A FOUR-STEP PROCESS TO MANAGING FEELINGS— THE *FITS* METHOD

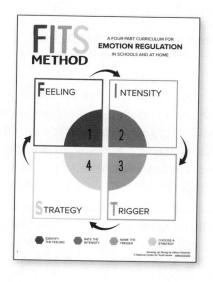

Several years ago, I was conducting a faculty training and a teacher asked, *"What would an ideal setup look like for schools to teach kids how to manage feelings?"*

My answer was simple: *"Every morning, each class would go through the four steps of emotional regulation as a group. Each day a different student would go through the steps and model using the steps in front of peers. This process would start in Pre-K and go all the way to 12th grade. When kids leave high school, they would know just as much about themselves as they would about the world around them.*" I added, "*If parents would do the steps daily at home, we could turn the tides of mental health in children.*" I believe this to be true.

Below are the four steps to emotional regulation, or the *FITS* Method:

The *FITS* Method

Step 1: Identify the FEELING

Step 2: Rate the INTENSITY

Step 3: Name the TRIGGER

Step 4: Choose a STRATEGY

Through the remainder of the chapter, I will share how to use the steps both at home and school so parents and educators can provide a wraparound approach for kids to learn these skills. I will also break the steps down into two stages: **Foundation Stage** (Ages 2-10) and **Growth Stage** (Ages 11-17) as children process emotion based on their developmental level of functioning.

FOUNDATION STAGE *(Ages 2-10)*	GROWTH STAGE *(Ages 11-17)*
Concrete Concepts	Abstract Concepts
Basic Emotions	Complex Emotions
Either/Or Thinking	Gray Thinking

In the Foundation Stage, children are just learning about emotions They are concrete thinkers, so the best way for them to learn is to <u>see</u> what emotions look like. They need a visual example of what angry looks like—the way your eyebrows tense up, your eyes squint, and your lips become tight. The same goes with happy—a smile appears on your face, the eyes are bright, the face is round.

FOUNDATION STAGE

They also need coping strategies to be taught in a concrete way. They need a Worry Jar to put their worries in or a pretend remote control to change negative thoughts to positive ones. The concrete representation of emotions helps children learn how to manage emotions at their developmental level.

GROWTH STAGE

In the Growth Stage, children can think abstractly about emotions. They see the gray in situations and can identify multiple emotions about the same event. For example, going to a school dance can be exciting, frightening, overwhelming, and disappointing all at the same time. During the Growth Stage, kids are learning who they are, separate from their parents and family. They are developing their own beliefs and feelings about the way they see themselves in the world. The Growth Stage is an exciting time to process emotions with kids because their minds are open, and their brains are processing information quickly.

The Growth Stage is also a critical time to learn emotional regulation as emotions are surging and kids have more access to unhealthy ways of managing emotions, such as substance abuse or self-harm.

Regardless of developmental stage, the most important factor in the *FITS* Method is repetition. When kids practice going through the steps every day, the process becomes second nature. Just as kids need to read every day to learn how words flow within sentences, they need to practice emotional regulation daily to understand how the steps flow within their lives. Life events will change, but the steps never change. The consistency of the steps will create an ease in managing feelings. Instead of focusing on the trigger of the feeling, kids will learn to focus on the steps, and the steps will lead to empowerment.

AT HOME
Teaching the *FITS* Method

As a parent or caregiver, you are the model for mental health for your children. The way you manage feelings will be the way your child learns to manage them. Many parents reading this book were not taught healthy ways to manage feelings as children. In this case, you will learn the steps alongside your own kids. That is not a bad thing. In fact, it can be quite useful to learn together. Be transparent with your child as you learn the steps together. Be willing to admit when you do not manage feelings appropriately and share your intention to do better. Kids enjoy being the teacher and telling you when you haven't followed the steps. Watch out! Once you start this process, kids will keep you in line.

Step 1: Identify the *FEELING*
(Ages 2-10)

The most effective way to teach young children to identify feelings at home is a strategy I call, **You Pick Three.** I recommend choosing a set of feeling cards to do this activity. The cards need to be fun and age-appropriate to help engage your child. The activity takes less than five minutes each day and is best incorporated into a bedtime routine.

Here are the steps:

1. Each evening, ask your child to choose three feelings from the deck of feeling cards to describe their day. For example, your child might say, *"I felt happy, sad, and angry today."* In this first step, your child is beginning to see their day through the lens of feeling. Instead of just telling you about events in their day, your child is sharing the feelings they experienced.

2. Now, you, as the parent, choose three feelings to share about your day. There are only two requirements here: 1) Always choose the feeling your child struggles with the most. For example, if your child is anxious, you will want to pick worried each day to normalize the feeling, and 2) Use the child version of the feeling, not the adult version. For example, identify feeling sad instead of depressed.

Some Things to Note: Your child may not choose the feeling they struggle with the most because 1) they are not aware of the feeling, or 2) they don't want to admit having the feeling. In this case, keep choosing the feeling they struggle with anyway. For example, if they struggle with worry, identify worry in your own day and then ask, "When *do you feel worried?"* Notice I did not ask *if* they feel worried because everyone feels worried at times. You're asking *when*, which lets them know you are aware of their worry and that helps them become aware of it as well.

(Ages 11-17)

At this age, your child can think abstractly so you do not necessarily need a visual example of feelings. Instead, you can talk about the feelings in their day. The best time to talk to teenagers about feelings is later in the evening. Just before bed, ask how they felt that day. Instead of asking, *"How was your day?"* ask, *"How did you feel today?"* If you are just starting this process, your child may skip over the feeling and go right to the events of their day. If this is the case, listen to the events but then ask how your child felt about the events. For example, if your teenager says, *"I got an A on the math test,"* you can say, *"That's great to hear! How do you feel about your grade?"* Maybe they were surprised, happy, or even confused as to how they did so well. In any case, this step will help them identify the feeling underneath the achievement.

Step 2: Rate the *INTENSITY*

(Ages 2-10)

The next step is to rate how "big" the feeling is from 1–10 (1 being the lowest and 10 being the highest). Your child has already picked their three feelings, now they are going to tell you how big each one is. The best way to implement this step with young children is to draw a number line and ask them to circle how big each feeling is. Every child's number line will look different. For some kids, a 10 is a tantrum and for other kids, it will be complete silence. Ask your child what a 10 looks like to them, then a 5, and then a 1. You may need to help your child think through this process as they may be unaware of how they are exhibiting emotions. In the example below you can see the child chose three feelings—calm, happy, and worried. They have circled the intensity of each feeling and have written the word above the number:

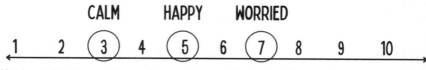

If the child doesn't want to write out their feelings above the number line, they can tell you how intense each feeling is verbally. Some kids also like to lay their feeling card above the appropriate number. All these options are fine.

Next, the parent rates the intensity of their feeling. For parents of big feelers, this step is important as it normalizes just how intense feelings can be. Kids at the Foundation Phase love to hear parents' struggles, so if you share feeling scared at a 10, kids will love coming to your aid. My three-year-old loves to hear I am afraid of stepping into the cold ocean. She holds my hand and tells me, *"The ocean is not scary, Mama. It's friendly."* She loves seeing I am afraid of things, too.

(Ages 11-17)

Adolescence is a time when feelings are elevated. Teenagers feel things deeply and intensely, so this step is very important in helping them understand how emotional intensity affects their daily lives. After your child shares their feeling in step one, ask them how intense the feeling is. In the first step, the example was, *"I feel surprised I got an A on the test."* Now ask, *"How surprised were you from 1–10?"* Kids in the Growth Stage will have a better idea of what 1–10 feels like than younger kids, so they should be able to tell you the intensity of their feelings without having to see them drawn on paper. The sharing of the intensity gives you a window into your teen's inner world you may not have had before. It also provides a way for you to understand their behavior. Many teens don't openly share the happenings in their day, which leaves parents to poke and prod them for information. When they share "I'm Feeling Angry at a 10," you know to give them some space. You may be able to discuss the reason later, but you know that you don't need to push the issue until your child's emotional intensity has lessened.

Step 3: Name the *TRIGGER*

(Ages 2-10)

This step is where kids learn what triggers their feelings. Kids in the Foundation Phase are in the beginnings of identifying what triggers their feelings, so this is a learning process. After your child has picked their three feelings and rated their intensity, it is time for them to tell you what has triggered the feeling.

An example of a child going through this third step is: *"I feel sad at a 7 because I can't go to the birthday party."*

As a parent, you are only listening during this third step. You are not pushing for more information nor are you confirming or denying your thoughts about their trigger. Instead, you are listening to your child's triggers and then saying, *"Thank you for sharing that with me."*

After your child names their triggers, it's time for you to name yours. During this step, refrain from sharing triggers that might add stress to your child. This is not a time for sharing your work or marriage stress. Choose benign triggers such as being late for work or stuck in traffic that will not cause your child to worry about your overall well-being.

(Ages 11-17)

Teens are much less likely to share their triggers than younger children. There will be things that occur in your teen's life that you will never really know. What's most important in this step is that your teen is aware of their own triggers. It's less about you as a parent and more about them. If your teen says they are sad at a 10 but doesn't want to say why, you can respond with, *"You must be feeling really sad. How can I support you?"* Teenagers have more opportunities to react to their triggers in negative ways, so offering your support is going to be the most useful thing for a child experiencing intense feelings.

As a parent, you can go into greater detail about your triggers with a child in the Growth Stage than you would with a younger child. If your teen seems distressed but isn't sharing their trigger you can say, *"I'm <u>worried</u> at a <u>10</u> because you don't open up to me anymore."* This demonstrates the first three steps in a non-confrontational way. Instead of saying, *"Why don't you talk to me anymore?"* which puts pressure on your teen, you are sharing your feelings about the situation, which is going to provide connection instead of confrontation.

When your teen does share their triggers, it's important not to overreact. If you do overreact, you will greatly decrease the chances they will share valuable information with you again. Refrain from overwhelming them with questions, threatening to call other parents or the school, or not allowing your teen to hang out with certain people. Consider it a privilege if your teen shares their triggers with you. Honor it and thank them for it. This will help them trust you and open up more. As they become adults, they will have a much greater likelihood of talking with you and sharing what is going on in their life.

Step 4: Choose a *STRATEGY*
(Ages 2-10)

Strategies are the bread and butter of emotional regulation. Strategies allow children to manage the feelings inside of them. When it comes to strategies, you don't need many. My five-year-old will close his eyes and take a deep breath when he needs to calm down. It helps him regulate his body and make a better choice. Kids in the Foundation Phase are just beginning to learn how to calm their minds and bodies so it's important to be patient with them in the process.

There are a variety of coping strategies for children at this age. The most important factor in choosing a strategy is that it is concrete. You can draw a heart on a piece of paper to show your child the steps to the **Color Your Heart Technique** [listed in the References section] to help your child process their feelings.

In this final step, your child can say, *"I felt <u>frustrated</u> at a 7 because Sarah wouldn't play with me. I chose the 'Cooked Spaghetti' technique* [listed in the Resources section] *to calm my mind and body."* I have included a FITS worksheet in the resource section that you can use as a guide through the steps. You can also print it out so your child can practice on their own.

As a parent, you can say, *"I felt <u>frustrated</u> at a 6 because I was stuck in traffic this morning. I also used 'Cooked Spaghetti' to calm my mind and body."* By sharing this, your child can see that you have big feelings that need to be managed and you are choosing the same strategy as them! This type of interaction will create a bond between you and your child around feelings. You are both equals, going through the process of regulating feelings together.

(Ages 11-17)

A teenager's ability to put these four steps together before college is paramount. If your teen can go through these steps on their own, they will be able to manage anything that comes their way. In this final step of identifying strategies, you can suggest strategies that are abstract as well as concrete. Different strategies will work for different kids but some common strategies for teens are as follows: exercise, yoga, meditation, taking a long bath, journaling, writing, and relaxation techniques.

A great way to connect with your teenager in the Growth Phase is to do coping strategies together. Many parents and kids will take a yoga or jujitsu class together. You can also go for a run, bike ride, or walk together. While doing a coping strategy together, it's important to focus on the positive effects you are getting for yourself, not just what your teen gets. For example, instead of saying, *"Don't <u>you</u> feel less stressed?"* after a yoga class, say, *"<u>I</u> feel less stressed."* This will help your child see the activity as less of a chore and more of an opportunity.

Unless teens learn to use positive emotion regulation strategies, they will resort to finding negative ones on their own. Overuse of technology, substance abuse, and self-harm are some examples of negative coping strategies teens use to manage overwhelming feelings. Getting ahead of the curve by teaching the four steps will reduce kids' need for negative coping strategies. Teens can take healthy coping strategies they learn in these formative years to college and beyond.

AT SCHOOL
Teaching the *FITS* Method

Many schools have at least one school counselor in place. Some schools have several school counselors, and others have none at all. Some schools are fortunate to have additional social workers and school psychologists to support the emotional needs of children. No matter the situation, one thing is for certain; **there is not enough emotional support in schools for children.** I started my counseling career as the sole school counselor to over 600 students. I taught weekly classes and offered support to those I could but there was never enough time. I have heard the same stories from other counselors. There is simply too much work to do in the area of emotional regulation for counselors alone. **This is why I believe emotional regulation needs to become part of the daily classroom routine, in every classroom, in every school.**

I need to mention here that I am a former teacher and know the time constraints and continual pressure on teachers. I am not suggesting that classroom teachers add another thing to their plate without getting something out of it. **What I am suggesting is that if you spend the five minutes it takes to implement the *FITS* Method each day, you will spend exponentially less time managing behavior and emotional issues.** Being a classroom teacher in the present day is more than teaching academics. It includes behavior management, emotional support, and even being a surrogate parent to children who lack stable adults in their lives, sad as that is.

FITS will help free up time for teachers by teaching emotional regulation on the front end, instead of putting out behavioral and emotional fires on the back end. It will not remove problems but will enable children, rather than their teachers, to solve problems on their own. It will give students the ability to challenge themselves, learn about what triggers their emotions, and develop healthy coping strategies to manage the academic, social, and emotional hurdles that are part of childhood. Ultimately, it will help teachers and students work together and communicate in meaningful ways.

Step 1: Identify the *FEELING*
(Ages 2-10)

Each morning during circle time or after students have completed morning work, go over visual examples of the types of feelings as a class. It's best if the feelings are posted on a board or wall where all students can easily see them. Say the feeling first, then ask the students to recite the feeling back to you. For example:

Teacher: "*Happy.*"
Class: (recites) "*Happy.*"
Teacher: "*Jealous.*"
Class: (recites) "*Jealous.*"

In the first two weeks of teaching *FITS*, you will want to explain what each feeling means. Spend time talking about how the face and body look when experiencing each feeling and ask the students to practice making the feeling faces along with you. After they learn what each feeling is, ask each student to share how they feel with the class.

Student: "*I feel happy this morning.*"

Then, ask the class, "*Does anyone else feel happy this morning?*" to normalize the feeling. At this age, students like to share information so you should have plenty of cooperation!

(Ages 11-17)

In the Growth Phase, most students are aware of what feelings look like and mean. Before class starts, ask the class if anyone wants to share how they are feeling that day. In some classes, you may have many students who want to share, and in other classes you might not have anyone who wants to share. In that case, the teacher can share how they are feeling that day, which models the identification and sharing of feelings. You will want to share something related to academics, like, *"I'm excited about sharing the new science project with you."* Then ask, *"Would anyone else like to share their feeling?"* to see if that brings about more willingness to share.

What you want to do in this first step is help students become aware of what they feel in the moment. This awareness helps them look inward at the way they process their school day, instead of outward at problems and situations. If students have learned the steps earlier in childhood, they will be adept at doing this already. If not, this may be a new, and much-needed, experience for them. By sharing their feelings with other students, they will see they are not alone.

Step 2: Rate the *INTENSITY*

(Ages 2-10)

Most students in the Foundation Stage have not yet learned how to rate the intensity of their feelings. The best way to teach this step is to draw out a number line for your students, like the one below:

$$1 \quad 2 \quad 3 \quad 4 \quad 5 \quad 6 \quad 7 \quad 8 \quad 9 \quad 10$$

Then, start with 10 and explain that this is when feelings are the biggest. Ask students in the class to share what happens when they are at a 10. Examples are crying, yelling, hitting, running away, etc. Then move to a five and share, *"This is when you can feel a feeling but can still control it."* Then move to a one and share, *"This is when you can barely feel a feeling."* Then, fill in the numbers in between, talking about what you might do when you feel each level of intensity.

Once you have established the number line and explained it, students will be able to readily share the intensity of their emotions. You can ask a student who has already shared their feeling how big their feeling is. For example:

Teacher: *"How happy do you feel, Milo?"*

Student: *"I feel <u>happy</u> at a <u>10</u> this morning!"*

Teacher: *"Does anyone else have a feeling that is a 10 this morning?"*

Student: (another student shares) *"I feel excited at a 10!"*

This helps normalize feelings and lets other students begin to think about how big their feelings are.

(Ages 11-17)

For students in the Growth Phase, you will also want to draw a number line to explain the intensity of emotions.

$$1 \quad 2 \quad 3 \quad 4 \quad 5 \quad 6 \quad 7 \quad 8 \quad 9 \quad 10 \longrightarrow$$

The classroom discussion will be much more advanced at this stage as students will be better at describing how each level of intensity feels. As with younger students, begin with a discussion about how intense a 10 might feel, then a five, then a one.

Ask a student to share how they are feeling, and how intense the feeling is.

Teacher: *"Is anyone willing to share their feeling and its intensity?*

Student: *"I feel sad at a 6 today."*

Teacher: *"Is anyone else feeling sad today?"*

Student: *"I also feel sad but it's at an 8."*

This step normalizes emotions and helps students connect and see that it's ok to feel all of the feelings. In the above example, students are connecting around their feeling of sadness. It's ok to feel sad, even necessary at times. When students see they are not alone, it reduces the sad feeling and increases the feeling of connectedness.

Step 3: Name the *TRIGGER*
(Ages 2-10)

Now it's time for students to share the reason for the feeling. At the Foundational Stage, kids are generally open about their triggers. An example is, *"I'm excited for my birthday!"* Another might be, *"I'm scared of spiders."* In this step, you ask a student to begin at step one and continue to step three. Like this:

Student: *"I feel <u>worried</u> at a <u>4</u> about going to sleep-away camp."*

This student can complete three of the four steps, which is more than most adults can accomplish! Now ask the class, *"Does anyone else feel worried today?"* Worry is an important feeling to normalize as many students are often afraid to admit the feeling. Worry and sadness are isolating feelings, as students will say, *"No one else worries like I do"* or *"No one else understands."* If another student identifies with worry, ask the student, *"Would you like to share what makes you feel worried?"* Many students worry about the same types of things so hearing that other student share the same struggles helps students feel less alone.

(Ages 11-17)

There are many triggers that adolescents are not comfortable sharing. In the Growth Stage, triggers become more complex and include social and emotional dynamics that are often hidden from parents and educators. When you ask students about their triggers, you may hear a variety of academic triggers such as workload, tests, college acceptance, overall grade point averages, and lack of sleep. These are common triggers in adolescence. You may not hear about the romantic and social triggers that are common at this stage, and that's ok. Work with what students bring to the table. For example:

Teacher: *"Would anyone like to share a feeling, its intensity, and the trigger?"*

Student: *"I feel <u>overwhelmed</u> at a <u>10</u> because of midterm exams."*

Teacher: *"Does anyone else feel overwhelmed about the exams?"*

You will likely get a big response to this type of question. Normalizing such a common stressor allows for classroom discussions about effective ways to manage stress. It also helps the class connect around a common trigger and helps educators better understand just how difficult the workload can be at times.

A Note about Triggers: If a student brings up a trigger or reaction to a trigger that causes alarm, pause the discussion and meet with the student after class to discuss. You want to create an open environment in your classroom, but you also don't want to exacerbate the intensity of emotions or give students unhealthy ideas about how to manage them. Alerting the school counselor, social worker, or administration will be an important step should such a situation arise.

Step 4: Choose a *STRATEGY*

(Ages 2-10)

Students in the Foundation Stage need to see concrete examples of how to manage feelings. Using strategies with students at this age is really fun! Students enjoy doing activities together and are generally open to learning what would help them manage their feelings. To do this final step, I would ask a student to come up to the board or front of the class and go through each step. For example:

Student: *"I feel excited at an <u>8</u> because we are going on a field trip today. I am going to use 'Shake My Sillies Out'* [listed in the Resources section] *to let my excited feelings out."* (As I mentioned previously in this chapter, I have included a *FITS* worksheet in the resource section that can be a guide for you to use with your students. You can also print it out for them to use so they can practice on their own.)

In this example, a student is sharing a positive feeling (excited) and is using a strategy to let the excess energy out. As educators, you know how special events such as field trips cause many feelings that often lead to a meltdown. After a child shares the four steps, the teacher could say, *"Is anyone else excited about the field trip today?"* I suspect unanimous agreement to this question. Then, *"Let's all stand up and Shake our Sillies Out together."* This use of the steps in *FITS* allows the teacher to get ahead of the probable student meltdown due to excess emotions. Instead of waiting until the collapse, doing *FITS* at the beginning of the class will help kids let their feelings out before the eruption.

(Ages 11-17)

This final step is paramount for students in the Growth Stage. Knowing how to channel feelings at this stage will help students learn to ride the waves of feelings without letting feelings take over their lives. Doing this final step as a class will help other students learn effective ways to manage the stressors of adolescence by using the most powerful form of learning in the Growth Stage— peer influence. For example:

Teacher: *"Would anyone like to come up to the board and go through the four steps of FITS?"*

Student: *"I feel <u>overwhelmed</u> at a <u>9</u> because I have four tests this week. I am going to do 'Focus for Fifteen'* [listed in Resource section] *to help get the work done but also give my brain the mental rest it needs."*

Teacher: *"Has anyone else tried 'Focus for Fifteen?' Would you like to share with the class how it went?"*

There are so many places you can go with students in the Growth Stage as you complete the steps. You can normalize the feeling by asking the class who feels the same way. You can talk about the intensity by asking who feels a 9 during a typical school day. You can discuss academic pressure by asking who else has four tests this week. You can also go over Focus for Fifteen again to refresh the strategy in their minds.

The ability of a student to go through the steps before finishing high school will greatly influence how they manage difficult feelings not only in college, but throughout their lives. As you go through the steps, you will find your conversations with students are different. Instead of students asking for more time to complete an assignment or expressing frustration about a specific task, they can share how they are feeling and how they are going to manage that feeling. As an educator, you are supporting them in their process. This helps students become accountable and educators become more empathetic to what students need. Together, this will help the student/ teacher relationship dramatically and shape the life of the student.

- **The *FITS* Method is a four-step approach to emotional regulation.**

- **There are two stages: Foundation Stage (Ages 2-10) and Growth Stage (Ages 11-17) based on a child's developmental level of functioning**

- **Parents and caregivers model mental health for children at home.**

- **Being a teacher these days includes behavior management, emotional support, and even being a surrogate parent to children.**

- **Training children to implement the *FITS* Method when they are young will lead to more emotional intelligence throughout their lives.**

KEY POINTS TO REMEMBER

CHAPTER FOUR

BUILDING EMOTIONAL MUSCLES

Usain Bolt, the fastest human on the planet, has an uneven stride. One would think he would have a perfect stride in watching him seemingly fly on the track. The research team at Southern Methodist University found that not only is his stride uneven, but one of his legs is half an inch shorter than the other and he has scoliosis. They went on to find that the compensation of his uneven stride is what has made him great. Michael Jordan was cut from his high school basketball team and went on to be arguably the greatest basketball player of all time. Jim Carrey dropped out of high school to support his family but never let go of his dream to become a comedian. At thirteen years old, Bethany Hamilton had her arm bitten off by a shark. Two years later she won a national surfing championship.

We love hearing stories like this because they inspire us and help us believe anything can happen. But behind these stories are great struggles and loads of emotional discomfort. The people who overcome great things are filled with doubt, fear, and anxiety, just like the rest of us. They just didn't quit. **We often see others doing hard things effortlessly, but what looks like effortlessness is the product of doing something with great effort time and time again.** It's only when we finally master something that it becomes effortless. Until then, we work, and we work, and we work. No one seems to notice the effort until we are successful, but we never become successful without the work.

SHORT-TERM DISCOMFORT = LONG-TERM COMFORT

One of the most important things we can teach kids is how to manage short-term discomfort. Only by managing short-term discomfort can a child reap the benefits of long-term comfort. Long-term comfort comes from mastering a task, accomplishing a goal, or feeling confident and capable of doing something difficult. Long-term comfort comes in knowing how to talk to someone new, solve a complex math problem, or give a speech in front of a classroom of peers. Long-term comfort is the ability to access emotional endurance when it matters most. But kids can only arrive at long-term comfort if they have the resilience to get through the beginning phases of something when it's hard and the rewards aren't coming easily.

Short-term discomfort begins at the start of something when it is new and most painful. If you want to get into shape, your first session with a personal trainer will be the hardest. If you want to find a romantic partner, the first few dates will be the most uncomfortable. For kids, short-term discomfort comes from being on a new sports team, moving to a new school, or taking a class that isn't in their area of strength. Sometimes, the desire for long-term comfort is so strong that kids will sign up for short-term discomfort.

When I was a kid, I wasn't quick and couldn't jump very high, but I loved basketball, so I learned how to shoot well enough to become a good player. I felt the short-term discomfort of keeping my elbow in, shooting for countless hours, and repeating my shooting routine every day for years. Some of my more naturally athletic teammates didn't practice and had more success, but my discomfort was worth it to be part of the team. The gains from basketball were much more than points scored and games won. It gave me the confidence to see that if I wanted something bad enough, I could work hard enough to get it. That confidence gave me more in life than basketball could ever give.

Alternatively, some kids don't sign up for short-term discomfort. They don't want to move schools, go to sleep-away camp, or join a sports team. They feel forced to do something hard and you will see much more resistance in this situation. Even so, there are great gains from doing something hard. I've worked with kids who were terrified of going to a new school but ended up loving it. I've worked with kids whose best friend moved away and they were terrified of being alone on the playground. By the end of the year, they had more friends than before and were happier. No matter the situation, no one enjoys short-term discomfort.

AT HOME
How to Help Kids Manage Short-Term Discomfort

As parents, you will see the biggest pushback when it comes to short-term discomfort. Kids will show a strong face outside of the home but will show great resistance once they feel safe in the home. It is hard to watch your child struggle, and the tendency to rescue them from short-term discomfort is hard to resist. If you can stay the course, however, you will find that your child will become stronger from enduring short-term discomfort. You will see the pain lessen as the new routine or situation becomes familiar and your child achieves social, academic, and emotional gains from pushing through the discomfort.

To support your child in managing short-term discomfort, it's important to do two things:

1. **Acknowledge the discomfort**
2. **Write out long-term goals with your child**

As a parent, acknowledging your child's pain is important. It's easy to skip over the pain and move right to the gain of the discomfort.

For example:

Child: *"I don't want to go to soccer practice tonight! I'm tired!"*

Parent: *"Those other kids are out there getting better. Don't complain if they get more playing time than you!"*

The parent in the above situation failed to acknowledge the discomfort in their child and moved right to the outcome. While what the parent is saying may be true, it does not acknowledge the difficulty and strength it takes to attend the practice. Try this instead:

Child: *"I don't want to go to soccer practice tonight! I'm tired!"*

Parent: *"I know it's really hard to do something when you're tired. If you stay home, will you achieve your goal?"*

Which brings us to Step 2: Write goals down with your child.

Goal-setting is such an important part of building emotional muscles because it helps children see the light at the end of the tunnel. When the pain is most intense, keeping sight of the goal will sustain your child. For example, sit down with your child at the start of a sports season or school year and ask them to write three goals down for the year. This could be things like: to make the Honor Roll, average 10 points per game, or make three new friends in class. Keep in mind that the goal is what the child, not the parent, desires.

Even if *your* goal is for your child to be a straight-A student, if that is not what your *child* desires, that goal won't have any value to your child. The way to help children develop awareness of who they are and what they want is to start this process early. Some kids want to make $100 selling lemonade in the front yard so they can buy a new bike. That's a great goal and will sustain your child when the weather gets hot and no potential buyers are in sight. When they achieve their goal, self-esteem, confidence, and emotional muscles are formed and a child can take their momentum from the lemonade stand and turn toward another challenging experience.

AT SCHOOL

How to Help Kids Manage Short-Term Discomfort

School comes with a variety of discomforts. All kids face the discomforts of academics, social situations, and overall stress during the school year. As educators, it's important for us to help students set goals at the beginning of each year. In the first week or two of school, sit down with each of your students to discuss their goals for the school year. Give them a couple of days' notice so they can think about what matters to them most.

Write down three goals and keep them concrete and measurable, such as:

- Make an A in math
- Turn assignments in on time
- Run for Student Council

These goals will help a student develop a clear focus on what they want to accomplish. When things get tough and they start falling behind, revisit the goals with the student and let them determine whether the goals are being met. If they aren't being met, develop a plan to help achieve the goals. This approach helps students feel like there is something to be gained from their school experience. Most educators tell students what is expected without any consideration of what the student expects of themselves. Holding students accountable for the goals they've set creates buy-in from students. It will also help them push through the hard times during the year because the goals are their own and are meaningful to them.

THE MENTAL HEALTH JOURNEY

A child's mental health journey is their own. We are there to provide emotional support, and to be professionals to assist and provide scaffolding, but ultimately it will be the child who chooses whether to use a coping strategy, make healthy decisions, or take advantage of the resources provided to them. Children often look to adults to fix problems, but as taught throughout this book, that is ultimately not going to help them.

As an adult, it's helpful to think of a child within an emotional hula hoop and yourself within your own hula hoop.

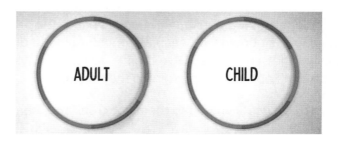

This will help you determine where the boundaries lie. You may be close by, but you can't make decisions for a child inside their hula hoop, and they cannot make decisions for you.

This realization is imperative if you are going to maintain your own mental health when a child struggles with theirs. Even as an educator, when you see a child struggle, the inclination is to relieve the discomfort so you don't have to worry about the child late at night when you should be sleeping. Early in my career, a teenager I was working with committed suicide. I saw him in my office on a Wednesday and on Friday night he took his life. I was devastated to find out the tragic news as I had no idea he was suicidal. He denied suicidal ideation, had never attempted, and seemed in good spirits. I ran that session over and over in my mind, looking for answers. Maybe there was something I missed? Something he said that alluded to his plans?

I was processing the event with a colleague who told me something wise. He said, *"Sometimes mental distress is malignant."* He went on, *"An oncologist isn't expected to cure every case of cancer. Why are you expecting yourself to heal every child?"* I thought about his comment and realized that, as helpers, we expect to heal those in need and hold ourselves to an unreachable bar. I don't know if I could have saved that child in my office, but, looking back, I did everything I could to help him with his mental health needs. I helped him identify feelings, taught him coping strategies, and encouraged him to make social connections.

Many parents I have worked with over the years have faced the same situation. Their child has struggled with a mental health issue, and they felt it was their job to rescue them. I have talked with educators who felt the same way. They felt responsible for the decisions of their students when there was nothing they could have done to change the outcome. There is a fine line between providing support and trying to do it for them. Ultimately, we need to teach children to manage their mental health by developing the ability to self-soothe. When the problem becomes too big for them, then we step in to provide outside resources such as counselors, psychologists or other medical professionals.

We know a problem is too big for a child when there are changes in behavior, psychosomatic complaints, or emotional distress. I use the **Rule of Three** to determine when we need to step in. The Rule of Three looks at the three areas in a child's life: Home, School and Friends. If a child is struggling emotionally in one area, such as school, you may want to read a book with a child about the issue, teach coping strategies and encourage them to talk with the school counselor. If they are struggling in two areas, such as home and school, it's time to talk to someone outside of school such as a pediatrician or psychotherapist. If a child is struggling in all three areas, you need to get help as soon as possible as there is no area in the child's life where they feel success.

HOME

SCHOOL

FRIENDS

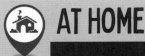

AT HOME

How to Teach Kids to Self-Soothe

Self-soothing begins in infancy. Sleep training and removing pacifiers and bottles are developmentally appropriate ways to help children soothe themselves. It is gut-wrenching to hear your child cry, begging you to come back to their crib, but necessary. Children need to learn to sleep on their own. Is it hard for them? Of course, but as my pediatrician once told me, *"You start teaching them about life the minute they are born."* And the great thing is, kids adjust. They cry it out and learn to sleep on their own. The ability to sleep on their own allows them to self-soothe and self-soothing teaches them how to manage discomfort. We are all wired to survive. We must give our kids a chance to do it.

As children become toddlers, we begin to set more boundaries. We say no. We don't give in to their every need because it's not good for them. A three-year-old doesn't know how much TV is too much or how much sugar will upset their stomach. They can't self-regulate so we regulate for them, allowing them to learn how to deal emotionally with a no. As kids get into elementary school, we widen our fence to allow them to experience school—not perfectly, but imperfectly. We don't give into our urge to request the nicest teacher in the grade. We don't contact the teacher twenty minutes after our child comes home with a bad grade. We start to trust that the lessons our child is learning are important, and, instead of intervening, we watch our child grow emotionally from these imperfect moments.

As they get into adolescence, we help them learn how to take care of themselves. We encourage them to use strategies and are willing to do them together. We offer to go to a yoga class with them or take a walk after dinner to help clear their head. By the time they leave our homes, they will have a clear idea of what they need to manage stress. As you can see below, the parental fence widens as children get older to allow them room to grow and develop.

GROWING UP STRONG

PARENTAL FENCE

TODDLERS

CHILDREN

ADOLESCENTS

Many first-year college students don't finish their first year because they are unable to self-soothe. In a dorm room with an unfamiliar roommate, difficult classes, and a blank social calendar, they have no idea how to manage the discomfort. Their calls home are gut-wrenching for parents, but if we teach them how to self-soothe before arriving at college they won't need parents as much. Parents will be a support, but not the sole support. The main support will be within themselves.

AT SCHOOL

How to Teach Kids to Self-Soothe

As educators, we also play a role in helping children self-soothe. We will see them struggle academically and socially, and our ability to allow them to struggle—while supporting them in the struggle—will allow them to build emotional muscles. If we reach out to parents as soon as the struggle begins, we remove the student's ability to learn to self-soothe and resolve problems on their own. We also remove the opportunity for students to self-advocate and resolve the issue with the help of the educator.

Students don't inherently know how to self-soothe when things become difficult at school. We must teach them. When they begin to feel emotional discomfort due to an academic or social concern, their first step in the self-soothing process should be to go through the *FITS* process of identifying the feeling, rating the intensity, naming the trigger, and choosing a strategy. One of the best strategies a student can use is to advocate for themselves by asking for the support of an educator.

You can teach children how to do this on the first day of school, as you are going over classroom rules and expectations. In grades K-5, you can teach this process by explaining to the class, *"If you are having a problem, you can raise your hand in class or come up to my desk during work time to ask for help."*

With older children, grades 6– 12, teach them how to write an email asking for additional support. Email is a very common way to communicate, especially as kids get older. If kids learn this skill in high school, they will have a better chance of communicating with a professor or future boss. To teach this strategy, you can say, *"It's important for you to learn to self-advocate. Self-advocate means the ability to communicate your needs. Let's look at how to write an email advocating for help:"*

Dear Mr./Ms. _____,

I am struggling with _____. I have tried _____, _____, _____, but I am still struggling. Is there a good time for me to meet with you to get some help?

Thank you,

_____

While being able to write an effective email is important, it is just as (if not more) important to teach kids how to ask for help face-to-face. A great way to teach this is to role-play how to have this conversation.

Ask a student to volunteer with a made-up problem. A sample role-play might go like this:

Student: *"Ms/Mr. _____, I am struggling with _____. Is there a good time that you can help me?"*

Teacher: *"Thank you for letting me know. I can meet with you during my office hours on Tuesday at 12:00. If that doesn't work for you, I can meet after school today for a few minutes."*

Student: *"Thank you. Today after school works well for me. I will see you then."*

School counselors are fantastic allies in this process. They can role-play this scenario in sessions with students to help them gain confidence and find the right words. Outside counselors and psychotherapists are also great options to help kids find effective ways to voice their concerns and develop confidence in asking adults for help. I spoke with a college student recently who went to her professor during office hours for help. She noted that she learned this skill in high school and has found it indispensable in getting the support she needs in college. She also mentioned that many of her peers have not learned this skill and are afraid of asking professors for help. This skill is not only imperative in her journey but in every journey. The ability to ask for help, clarify information, and communicate effectively is a life-long skill.

EMOTIONAL SEQUENCING

If we think about what a child needs by the time they leave our homes and schools and work backward, we can see a path to them gaining emotional independence. I call this **emotional sequencing**, and it is a strategic plan to get kids where they need to be before they leave home. In this section, we are going to identify three goals you have for a child you teach, counsel or parent. Then we will make a plan for how to teach these skills before they leave high school.

Think about three life-skills goals you have for a child by the time they graduate from high school. If you are a parent, some goals might include doing a load of laundry, making a doctor's appointment, boarding an airplane, or being able to attend a party responsibly. If you are an educator, they might include learning effective study habits, time management, or test-taking strategies. As a counselor, you might have the goal of enabling a child to do the FITS steps on their own, knowing self-regulation skills, or knowing how to reset their brain.

Now, think about an effective plan for how to teach these skills in a timely manner. One parent I work with required her child to attend a three-week program the summer before her senior year of high school. She was an only child and had never been to sleep-away camp. Her mother didn't want her first experience being away from home to be her freshman year of college. This parent was using emotional sequencing to prepare her child for the world that awaited her. Other parents have booked plane flights to see relatives in other states and allowed their teen to go through security, to the gate, and check a bag alone so they would know how the process works before they had to manage it for the first time alone.

Now think of a plan for each skill you are trying to teach a child. If you feel stuck, you can always come back to this later. Take your time and think about how and when you want to teach the skill and what you hope to see a child accomplish by learning the skill.

It's important to share the value of these skills with a child. You want them to know you want to prepare them for the future because you care about them and want to see them succeed. Some kids will be fearful to do some of these skills at first. You may have to take small steps toward the goal if you feel resistance. That's why it's good to start early in the process. It may take some time to build resistance. Mike Riera, in his book, *Staying Connected to Your Teenager* shares that in adolescence, kids are going from regressed child to emergent adult. They fluctuate between the two modes of operation throughout the day.[9]

The regressed child fears the world and longs to stay in the comfort of home. The emergent adult is excited about the world and wants to prove mature enough to handle it. No matter where you find a child, it's important to remember that teenagers are afraid to leave home. It's scary to take the leap, but one way we can help with this transition is to give them a taste of the world ahead by allowing them to learn these skills while they are still in the comfort of our homes and schools. This will ease the transition and give them a good foundation from which to spring forward.

STRETCHING WITHOUT BREAKING

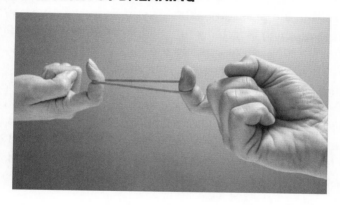

I like to use the example of a rubber band to talk about stretching kids to do hard things. A rubber band can be stretched, but, at some point, if it stretches too much it will break. We need to be careful when stretching kids so that we do not stretch past the breaking point. This is a fine line, but below are three examples of instances when children are stretched too much or stretched ineffectively.

1. When we push kids to meet our goals, instead of theirs
2. If psychosomatic complaints are present (stomachaches, headaches, etc.)
3. When mental health disorders are present and intense

When We Push Kids to Meet Our Goals, Not Theirs

I'll begin with number one as it is the primary reason for pushing children. It's hard sometimes to see our goals for our children versus their goals for themselves. I have met with many parents over the years who insist they are not pushing their children academically. They share they have never said their child needed to do well in school even though they themselves went to prestigious colleges and have competitive jobs. Here's the thing: you don't have to say you want your child to do something for your child to know it's expected. Children are like horses; they can sense where the pressure is. If you value education, your child will sense that they should too. If you value sports, your child will sense that as well.

How do you undo unspoken messages? The first thing is to recognize that the pressure is there even if you've never verbalized it. The second thing is to tell your child that everyone has different strengths and that you're open to them focusing on whichever strength they are most drawn to. This will acknowledge your awareness of the pressure and give your child the freedom to choose what matters most to them. This does not mean you allow your child to not try in school or meet expectations. Instead, it means that you understand they are different from you and may want different things. Success shows up in many ways, and it just might surprise you where your child ends up finding it.

Psychosomatic Complaints

When feelings are suppressed, they will manifest in the body, causing tension. If you are seeing habitual stomachaches and headaches in your child, you know there is stress in the body that is not being released. If this is the case, it's time to take a step back and reevaluate how important the stress is. For example, if your child signed up for a sleep-away camp but a week before it starts begins throwing up from anxiety, your child is being stretched too much. The body is so triggered by the event that it is removing everything inside in preparation for survival. You will want to take a step back and start with a sleepover at a close friend or relative's house to begin building the emotional muscles it takes to spend a whole week away.

When Mental Health Disorders Are Present

As I mentioned earlier in this book; if your child is struggling with a mental health disorder, it's as if they are walking up an emotional hill. They're tired and have used up more energy than other kids. In this case, you will want to push less than you would normally. Because life stressors are more intense if you have mental health disorder, you are going to take baby steps in making progress. Baby steps are still steps, moving in the right direction. For example, if your child struggles with social anxiety, you will still encourage them to go to a social event, but you can offer to pick up a friend to go with them. Here you are making progress toward the step of building emotional muscles, but you are providing extra support along the way.

- Only by managing short-term discomfort, can a child reap the benefits of long-term comfort.

- Emotional Sequencing is a strategic plan to get kids where they need to be before they leave home.

- We need to be careful when stretching kids so that we do not stretch past the breaking point. This can happen when we push kids to meet our goals, instead of theirs, if psychosomatic complaints are present, and when mental health disorders are present and intense.

- A child's mental health journey is their own. We are there to provide emotional support, professionals to assist and scaffolding, but ultimately it will be the child who chooses whether to use a coping strategy, make healthy decisions, or take advantage of the resources provided to them.

KEY POINTS TO REMEMBER

WHAT IS SUCCESS?

To simplify the concept of emotional success in childhood, it is **the ability to manage discomfort, push through emotional setbacks, and achieve hard things.** Notice that I didn't mention getting into a dream college, being homecoming queen, or getting an athletic scholarship. Going through the developmental stages of childhood, facing the adversity life brings, and surviving it, means success. Many kids have had great difficulties in childhood and overcome them. Other kids have seemingly breezed through K–12 and get out of high school and crash. A teenager who has struggled socially recently said, *"At least I am not peaking in high school."* By that she meant *the* **best is yet to come.** For many who are smart, attractive, and athletic, seemingly having it all, there will be hard times ahead of them. They will just have no experience in managing the discomfort that stems from them.

When parents ask me what type of child I worry most about, **it is the child who has not struggled.** Knowing how to read before you get into kindergarten, running the field in soccer, having lots of friends, and having kind, loving teachers throughout school can be a recipe for disaster. I believe the best recipe for childhood is this: **the family structure should be stable and consistent. The world outside should be challenging.**

If **parents** model emotional health and provide stable and consistent support, the child can face adversity and become emotionally strong in childhood. I've worked with parents who have gotten divorced, moved to several cities, had their houses burn down, and had family members die, but still maintained emotional health for their children. It is not the structures of homes and schools that sustain kids. It is the predictable adults in their lives, those who offer continual support through difficult times, whose influence endures.

If you are an **educator** reading this, you are valued more than you know. You spend more time with kids than their parents do, and you are an important role model of how an adult behaves in the world. Kids don't see their parents at work, but they see you at work and how you handle the ups and downs of the teaching profession. The respect you give students, your ability to manage your own emotions, and the consistency you offer day in and day out will be what guides students in their academic endeavors. I worked with an extremely anxious teenager who told me that every day she walked into school and told herself, "I just have to make it to 3rd period." What was so special about 3rd period? She had her favorite teacher. The one who made her laugh and helped her relax while teaching her interesting information. Teachers matter and kids are watching. Don't underestimate your value. Kids may not remember what they learned but they will always remember who taught them.

For you **counselors** out there, you have my heart. I began my career as a school counselor, and it remains my most rewarding job. I know you have a large caseload with more kids than you could possibly see. I know how hard you are working to meet the needs of students and there never seems to be enough time to get everything done. Yet, you are consistently there for students, to listen and encourage, to guide and teach skills. You may be the closest thing to a parent that many kids have. They look forward to seeing you because you give them unconditional, positive regard every time you see them. Keep showing up. Keep teaching skills. Even if they don't say it, you mean the world to kids.

RESOURCES

FITS WORKSHEET

Step 1: Identify the *FEELING*

MY FEELING:

ANGRY	BRAVE	CALM	CONFIDENT	CONFUSED	DISAPPOINTED	EXCITED
FRUSTRATED	HAPPY	HOPEFUL	JEALOUS	LONELY	OVERWHELMED	PROUD
SAD	SCARED	SHY	SILLY	SURPRISED	WORRIED	

Step 2: Rate the *INTENSITY*

1 2 3 4 5 6 7 8 9 10

Step 3: Name the *TRIGGER*

_____

Step 4: Choose a *STRATEGY*

_____

GROWING UP STRONG

COPING STRATEGY

POWER ROCK

WHAT YOU NEED:

Rock and markers or paint

HOW IT WORKS:

Ask a child to choose a rock from outside. It doesn't have to be any certain shape but small enough to fit in their pocket. Then, ask them to write or paint something that makes them feel happy or strong. Let the child make it their own but be willing to help if they ask. Then tell them when they feel sad, worried or lonely, they can hold onto their rock to remind them of how strong they really are. Then, ask them to choose a few words they can say to themselves while they are holding the rock. Statements such as, *"I am strong,"* or *"my mom will be waiting for me after school,"* are some examples. Ask the child to try the strategy with you so they can practice how it works.

WHY IT WORKS:

Kids are concrete thinkers and having something concrete to hold to helps them process positive statements and beliefs about themselves. The Power Rock can be taken anywhere a child goes and can be a tangible reminder of the strength they have inside. Power Rocks are also good to squeeze for five seconds and then relax for five seconds. This helps the body release tension and relax.

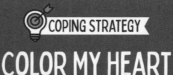
COPING STRATEGY

COLOR MY HEART

WHAT YOU NEED:

Paper and crayons or markers

HOW IT WORKS:

Ask a child to choose colors to identify their feelings. For example, blue for sad, yellow for happy, and red for angry. Then draw an outline of a heart and ask them to color it based on how much of each feeling they have. If they are feeling mostly sad, their heart will be mostly blue. If they are mostly happy, it will be mostly yellow and so on. Then, ask the child to explain what feeling each color represents and why they are feeling that way.

WHY IT WORKS:

This strategy helps children share their feelings in a safe way. Instead of having to explain their feelings in words, kids can show others what is happening inside of them. This strategy works especially well with young kids who don't have the verbal ability to share their emotions. It also works well with children who have a hard time opening up, and who struggle to put words to what is happening to them internally. I have used this strategy in counseling sessions for many years. Parents have also found it useful to help a child share how they are feeling. Teachers can also use this as a supplemental exercise while using the *FITS* Method in a classroom.

COOKED SPAGHETTI

WHAT YOU NEED:

A package of uncooked spaghetti and a small amount of cooked spaghetti

HOW IT WORKS:

Take out a piece of uncooked spaghetti and talk about how rigid it is. Apply some pressure to it and watch it break. Say to a child, *"You see how this cooked spaghetti couldn't handle much pressure?"* Now, choose a piece of cooked spaghetti and talk about how flexible it is. You can allow a child to touch it and move it around. Then say, *"When I add pressure, see what happens to the cooked spaghetti. It doesn't break, it just bends."*

Then share how our bodies become stiff and rigid when we feel stress. If we calm our bodies by breathing, we can become more flexible, just like cooked spaghetti. Ask the child what other activities might calm the body, i.e., yoga, reading, meditation, and exercise.

WHY IT WORKS:

This strategy gives kids a concrete example of how stress affects the body. It shows spaghetti breaking versus bending and helps kids identify what will help them bend, rather than break. This activity works fabulously in a counseling group, as a classroom lesson, or at home while cooking spaghetti with a parent. Later, after a child has learned the activity, you can ask, *"Are you feeling like cooked spaghetti or uncooked spaghetti?"* and they'll know just what you mean!

SHAKE MY SILLIES OUT

WHAT YOU NEED:

A free space to move

HOW IT WORKS:

Explain to a child, *"There are a lot of feelings that we keep in our bodies that sometimes need to come out. When we feel silly, our feelings come out even when we need to be quiet or sitting still. A good way to help our bodies calm down is by shaking our sillies out. Let's shake our silly feelings out by moving our bodies in silly ways."* Demonstrate for a child how to move their faces and bodies in silly ways.

WHY IT WORKS:

When kids feel silly or excited, their feelings often come out during structured times when they need to be quiet or sit still. It is often hard for kids to sit still during these times, but if they have an opportunity to release their energy *before* they need to sit still, they will have much more success. This is a great activity to do in a classroom before kids need to sit for a long period of time. It is also great to practice in a counseling session or at home to help children learn what to do with emotional energy.

FOCUS FOR FIFTEEN

WHAT YOU NEED:

A timer

HOW IT WORKS:

Tell a child their brain needs to take breaks to help them maintain focus and get work completed. Ask a child to set a timer for fifteen minutes and during that time, they are to work only. No phones, no screens, no distractions. At the end of fifteen minutes, they set the time for five minutes and during this time, they can stretch, take a walk or respond to a message. After the five minutes, they continue the fifteen-minute segments until they have completed their work.

WHY IT WORKS:

Breaking large tasks into bite-size pieces allows the mind to calm down and focus more clearly. Fifteen-minute increments allow for a steady flow of focus but then a short break allows the mind to wander and rest. This strategy has worked fabulously for kids who have heavy academic caseloads, limited time to do work or tend to become overwhelmed by deadlines.

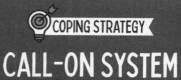

CALL-ON SYSTEM

WHAT YOU NEED:

5 minutes to meet with a student

HOW IT WORKS:

Say to a student, *"It seems you're worried about raising your hand in class. Classroom participation is a requirement for our class but here's an idea. If you agree to raise your hand at least once each class period, I will agree to not call on you. How does that sound?"*

WHY IT WORKS:

Being called on in class is one of the biggest worries students have. If you see a child struggling to speak out in class, this strategy will help them gain confidence by speaking out when they know the answer or when it feels comfortable to them. This strategy is very useful for classroom teachers. It can also be facilitated by a counselor. As a parent, you can recommend that your child request this strategy from the teacher to ease worry in the classroom setting. It has been very successful for students of all grades, in a variety of settings.

I AM FEELING...

WORRIED → Rewrite the Story

SAD → Make a Good Things Jar

ANGRY → Ask for a Reset Time

EXCITED → Shake My Sillies Out

FRUSTRATED → Cooked Spaghetti

OVERWHELMED → Focus for Fifteen Minutes

ANYTIME → List Something You Can See, Hear, Smell, Taste, and Touch

ENDNOTES

1. VandenBos, G. R. (Ed.). (2015). APA dictionary of psychology (2nd ed.). American Psychological Association.

2. Edwards, Allison. 2021. Flooded: A Brain-based Guide to Help Children Regulate Emotions.

3. "College Student Mental Health Statistics | BestColleges," BestColleges.com, n.d., https://www.bestcolleges.com/research/college-student-mental-health-statistics/.

4. Jessica Booth, "Anxiety Statistics and Facts," Forbes Health, October 23, 2023, https://www.forbes.com/health/mind/anxiety-statistics/.

5. Mental Health UK, "Types of Anxiety Disorders - Mental Health UK," May 10, 2023, https://mentalhealth-uk.org/help-and-information/conditions/anxiety-disorders/types/#:~:text=Generalised%20anxiety%20disorder%20(GAD),about%20different%20activities%20and%20events.

6. Joshua Fitch, Senior Editor, "Navigating School-based Mental Health Services," *Contemporary Pediatrics*, February 28, 2024, https://www.contemporarypediatrics.com/view/navigating-school-based-mental-health-services.

7. Kyle Benson, "The Anger Iceberg," The Gottman Institute, March 5, 2024, https://www.gottman.com/blog/the-anger-iceberg/.

8. JT Cacioppo and S Cacioppo. *The growing problem of loneliness. Lancet. 391, no. 10119 (February 2016): 426.*

9. Michael Riera, Staying Connected to Your Teenager: How to Keep them Taking to You and How to hear What They're Really Saying. (Boston: Da Capo Lifelong Books, 2017).

DOWNLOADABLE RESOURCES AND TEMPLATES

Please visit **ncyi.org/growingupstrong** and click Downloadable Resources. Enter the code below in the form to download the file to your device.

STRONG560

ABOUT THE AUTHOR

Allison Edwards is a Licensed Professional Counselor, Registered Play Therapist, educational consultant, parent coach, creator and owner of All the Feels Company and author of numerous books including *Worry Says What?*, *Flooded*, and *15-Minute Counseling Techniques that Work*. Allison earned her graduate degree in Counseling from Vanderbilt University and has over 20 years experience working as a school teacher, school counselor, child/adolescent psychotherapist, Vanderbilt University professor and educational consultant to schools throughout the country.

ALSO AVAILABLE BY ALLISON

Flooded

A Brain-Based Guide to Help Children Regulate Emotions

When your brain perceives danger, your body and mind will go instantly into one of three modes-flight, fight, or freeze. Your heart races, your body tenses up, your hands shake, and your emotions take over rational thought.

You've entered The Flood Zone. Educators, counselors, and parents will learn to identify The Flood Zone, along with strategies for teaching children (and adults!) how to regain control of their emotions.

15-Minute Counseling Techniques that Work

What You Didn't Learn in Grad School

Children come to us with a variety of problems, searching for answers. While these solutions may work temporarily, we really never help children until we give them tools—or techniques—to manage thoughts and feelings on their own. The techniques in this book will help children feel empowered to face everyday challenges and equipped to manage their stress and emotions.

364 Days Until Halloween

Does Halloween Have You Spooked?

Halloween jitters? Don't worry, little monster!

Join Kai on a heartwarming journey through the changing seasons as he learns to embrace the magic of Halloween. Filled with vivid rhymes and whimsical illustrations, this delightful story celebrates friendship in unlikely places and the courage it takes to face your fears.

Marcy's Having All the Feels

Marcy wanted to be happy. But all her other feelings kept showing up—and at the worst times! Her feelings follow her around throughout the day. Then one day when Marcy's feelings disappear, she learns that her feelings don't have to control her, and they might even have a function. Maybe having all the feels might not be such a bad thing. And that one discovery? Well, it changes everything!

Worry Says What?

"Worry's songs tie my tummy up in knots. Sometimes he speaks in a whisper, and other times his voice gets so loud I can't hear anything else." This book shows how worry whispers to young minds, and offers a powerful tool all children can use to silence those fears.

Beat, Beat, Thump

What does anxiety feel like to a child? Beat, beat, thump. Beat, beat, thump. That's the pulse of Alex's heart as he navigates worries about school, friendship struggles, and trying new things. Sometimes the pounding of his heartbeat gets so loud that it's all he can hear.

How to Crack Your Peanut
Solving the Mystery of Why You Sometimes Lose Your Mind

Diego doesn't understand why he always seems to lose his temper and lash out at people.

This book is a gentle introduction to emotion regulation and helps kids understand how the brain works and how they can begin to listen to their bodies and control their emotions.

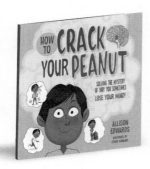

About NCYI

National Center for Youth Issues provides educational resources, training, and support programs to foster the healthy social, emotional, and physical development of children and youth. Since our founding in 1981, NCYI has established a reputation as one of the country's leading providers of teaching materials and training for counseling and student-support professionals. NCYI helps meet the immediate needs of students throughout the nation by ensuring those who mentor them are well prepared to respond across the developmental spectrum.

Connect With Us Online!

@nationalcenterforyouthissues

@ncyi

@nationalcenterforyouthissues